RAISED

HUNTING™

DAVID & KARIN HOLDER
with LARRY DUGGER

HARVEST HOUSE PUBLISHERS
EUGENE, OREGON

Cover design by Bryce Williamson

Cover photo by David and Karin Holder

Other cover images © ShutterWorx; phochi; Khjaproduction / Getti Images

Published in association with WordServe Literary Group, Ltd., www.wordserveliterary.com.

RAISED HUNTING is a trademark of Raised Hunting LLC. Harvest House Publishers, Inc., is a licensee of the trademark RAISED HUNTING.

Raised Hunting
Copyright © 2019 by David Holder, Karin Holder, and Larry Dugger
Published by Harvest House Publishers
Eugene, Oregon 97408
www.harvesthousepublishers.com

ISBN 978-0-7369-7767-8 (pbk.)
ISBN 978-0-7369-7768-5 (eBook)

Library of Congress Cataloging-in-Publication Data

Names: Holder, David (Hunter), author. | Holder, Karin, author. | Dugger, Larry.
Title: Raised hunting / David and Karin Holder ; with Larry Dugger.
Description: Eugene, Oregon : Harvest House Publishers, [2019] | Based on
    television show: Raised Hunting.
Identifiers: LCCN 2018061345 (print) | LCCN 2019000900 (ebook) | ISBN
    9780736977685 (e-book) | ISBN 9780736977678 (pbk.)
Subjects: LCSH: Hunting--United States. | Bowhunting--United States. |
    Hunting--Religious aspects. | Cooking (Game)
Classification: LCC SK41 (ebook) | LCC SK41 .H65 2019 (print) | DDC
    639/.1--dc23
LC record available at https://lccn.loc.gov/2018061345

Printed in the United States of America

19 20 21 22 23 24 25 26 27 / VP-SK / 10 9 8 7 6 5 4 3 2

I have a cross in my pocket and a bow in my hand. I believe hunting and life can be summed up in three words: Never give up.

DAVID HOLDER

CONTENTS

THE STORY BEHIND THE BOOK

BY LARRY DUGGER

Your life is a story. It sends the clear and often unspoken message of who you are and what you value. If you ask me, a life without an intriguing storyline is no life at all. The plot twists you weren't expecting and the unforeseen cast of characters spin the grandest tales. The stories in this book are some of the best I've heard—and not because I helped shape them but because, like David and Karin Holder, I believe our greatest adventures are found outdoors.

I was born and raised in the Ozark mountains of Missouri. Consequently, my love for hunting and all things outside began early in life. My fondest childhood memories revolve around long, lazy days spent swimming in the creek and time connecting with my family on hunting excursions. Being outside meant more to me than just not being inside. It was and still is where I feel most alive.

Like the Holders, I feel the responsibility to pass on my love for enjoying God's handiwork to the next generation. Chances are good that I wouldn't be who I am today if I hadn't spent many summer nights catching fireflies with my grandpa or tramping through the woods on a hunt with my dad and brother. If you ask me, we need more time in front of the campfire and less time in front of our electronic devices. A lot of our problems could be solved if we would take the time to relax, breathe in God's fresh air, and perhaps roast a marshmallow or two!

Being outdoors strengthens my relationship with God. This comes as no surprise to me. After all, He did create the earth for His most prized creation to enjoy. Every tree began as a seed that He planted. He poured the rivers out of the palms of His hands. Even the rocks were strategically placed by our Creator. The sunrise gets fresh paint every morning because we have a God who loves the beauty of a new day as much as we do!

I remember one hunt in particular that perfectly illustrates this point. It was opening morning of deer season, and I was sitting on top of a big hill that overlooked a valley where two ridges came together at the bottom, creating the perfect deer funnel. My family and I were hunting a buck we had named "Buck Norris." This deer was the big one we were all hoping to take down.

As I sat there in a makeshift hunting blind composed of a few scruffy cedar trees, I noticed a bald eagle circling just above my head. He and I were apparently eyeing the same red squirrel playing in the walnut tree out in the open field. The eagle was looking for breakfast. I was trying to pass the time while I waited for Buck Norris to show up. A flock of wild turkeys were drinking from a pond to my right, and a group of does had just exited the timber on my left.

It was spitting snow, and the sun was coming up behind me. In that moment, surrounded on every side by nature, I had never felt closer to God. There was no sermon, choir, or worship song. It was just Jesus and me. Don't get me wrong—I love going to church and rarely miss (which is a good thing, because I'm the pastor), but I can honestly say that hunting or anything related to the outdoors reminds me of the One who not only gave the outdoors to me but also gave His life for me.

You may be wondering how on earth a pastor and author from Missouri connected with David and Karin Holder, stars of the *Raised Hunting* TV show that airs on the Discovery Channel.

It was a typical Saturday morning at my house. My teenage sons were still sleeping, and my wife was sitting upstairs in her recliner, recovering from a week of teaching kindergarteners. I was downstairs making coffee. She said, "You really need to come up here and watch this hunting show." I was surprised because even though she hunts, she rarely watches outdoor television. "It's more than a hunting show," she added. "I really like this family. They aren't just killing stuff; they're teaching life lessons and talking about God. I think you'll like it."

I went upstairs and sat down. That was the first time I saw David and Karin Holder. I could tell right away that my wife was right. The Holders were far more than hunters. They were teachers and people of strong faith.

Then it happened…

You could call it an impression or perhaps information from God. I wasn't completely sure, but I felt like I heard an inward voice speak to me and the voice said, "I want you to help the Holders write a book." Shocked, I looked at my wife and told her what had just happened.

"What are you going to do?" she asked.

I didn't really know, but I decided to check out the *Raised Hunting* website to see if there was any contact information. Sure enough, there was an email address. I quickly sent an email, explaining who I was and asking David and Karin if they had ever thought about writing a book. If so, I would be glad to help.

A few days went by, and I honestly thought nothing would come from my request. You can't imagine how excited I was when Karin emailed me back. She said they had talked about writing a book but didn't know where to start. They'd been praying that God would help them. We arranged for me to come to their home in Iowa to discuss what a hunting book by the Holders might look like.

After a long conversation with David and Karin, we decided to team up on the material in this book.

This book is more than just a good idea; it's a God idea. My prayer for you is that you will be as inspired by the Holder family as my wife and I have been. David and Karin (and their sons, Warren and Easton) truly care about their viewers—and now their readers. This is the kind of book that invites you to buckle up and hold on. You are embarking on an outdoor adventure that will take you past hunting and into the life God has prepared for you.

THIS IS US

DAVID | If I'm not out bowhunting, I'm preparing to. If I'm not preparing, I'm talking about a bow hunt. And if you happen to catch me during one of those rare instances when I'm not talking at all…you can bet I'm thinking about the animal, the draw, and the moment when it all comes together.

As far back as I can remember, all I've ever wanted to do was spend every waking moment in the outdoors. At the age of 16, I discovered a bow and arrow. I became obsessed not only with the hunt but also the desire to learn everything possible about my prey. Since then, I've taken more than 200 animals with my bow. Don't get me wrong—I have no problem with guns or any other weapon. I just find the contest between man and animal to be much more personal from inside 40 yards.

My wife, Karin, and our two boys, Warren and Easton, share my passion. When we take family trips, we just happen to take our bows with us. Leisurely walks become scouting trips or searches for shed deer antlers. We do more than eat at our table. We check trail-camera pictures, discuss wind direction, and talk about our next hunting adventure. The defining part of my life—and Karin's and the boys'—is that we were all raised hunting.

I couldn't be happier as a husband, father, Christian, and American.

The Holder family after a successful antelope hunt. From left to right: Karin, David, Warren, and Easton Holder.

KARIN | I am a proud mother, Christian, and hunter. Like David, I was raised hunting, but because I was a girl, I wasn't expected to be a hunter—especially not a bowhunter. It wasn't until I met David that, with his encouragement, I began my hunting career. It's hard to believe I took my first deer more than 20 years ago.

My family is tightly woven into the outdoors. Some of our fondest memories have been created while hunting. David and I feel as though we're closer to our sons because of our outdoor lifestyle. And I have to say it's very special to see how excited the boys get when Mom "bags the big one."

I've been bowhunting now for close to two decades and have been blessed to take several animals and multiple species with archery gear and a muzzleloader. A lot of men and women have commented to me that they don't expect to see a professional woman like me out hunting. I truly hope that through this book you will see what a spectacular impact hunting can have on you and your family. Who knows? Maybe someday we'll share a camp.

Enjoy the book…and make the kids do the field dressing!

INTRODUCTION

DAVID | My outdoor journey probably began a lot like yours. I didn't have hundreds of acres to hunt or access to the kind of deer you see hanging in a trophy room. In the beginning, I hunted on public land and knocked on a lot of doors just to have a place to go. I did everything I could on my own with a very small budget. Why? Because I loved all things outdoors, and I still do.

Through years of hard work, Karin and I now have a piece of ground in Iowa where—I'm not going to lie—the deer are huge. I'm living the dream, but it didn't come easy. Nothing worth having usually does.

My family and I have a television show called *Raised Hunting*, which allows us to share our passion for the outdoors with others. This book is our journey. I'm inviting you to go behind the scenes and learn what it's like to be a part of the *Raised Hunting* family.

Every bowhunter knows what it means to pull back the bow and reach full draw. You're poised to make the shot. Hit or miss, you've done everything possible to position yourself for success. The hunt is the adventure, but you'll never reach the ultimate goal of taking an animal until you reach a full draw position. In life, you can position yourself to succeed in the stuff that really matters. You can learn to live at full draw.

In the following pages you're going to be taken places most people only dream about. You'll find that, most of the time, it wasn't the killing of an animal that changed our lives but that I got to hug my wife on the side of a mountain or watch an amazing sunset with my boys. Sharing those moments meant more than any antler ever will.

Everyone has at least one inherent gift from God, something unique to that individual. Recognizing and embracing our gifts will determine if we struggle or move on fairly well. I discovered pretty early in my life that I've been given a gift to hunt, a gift not just for my family and me to enjoy but to share. That's why we have a television show and why we have written this book.

David Holder

I've learned in my 50 years that true fulfillment is a successful life, not a successful hunt, but if you can find a way to bring those two together, you've got something to smile about.

You can learn to be a great hunter, but you can also learn to be a great dad, spouse, friend, and child of God. Life, like hunting, is best when I give it my full effort. You, too, can live at full draw in both life and on the hunt! Are you ready?

WHAT TO EXPECT

Every chapter is broken down into five easy-to-read sections. Each is designed to help you get to full draw spiritually, physically, mentally, and on the hunt. Read each section carefully and use the information illustrated in my family's outdoor adventures to help you be your best.

- *On the Hunt.* If you like the *Raised Hunting* television program, you'll love this. Join Karin and me as we take you behind the scenes on some of our most memorable experiences in the outdoors. We also share details about our family life—details that aren't included in the show.

- *Beyond the Hunt.* Spending time in the outdoors has taught us that everything we do can reveal a life lesson. The things that make us good hunters are often the same things that make us good spouses, parents, and friends. Karin and I are Christians, and our faith is very important to us. Here, we offer our best advice about how to take your life to the next level.

- *Anchor Points.* The most crucial part of the shot isn't drawing back your bow—it's the anchor point. If you're not anchored in precisely the same spot every time, your arrow will likely miss the target. Your success depends on a fixed anchor. Each chapter has a summary of points that will help you remember key details. Use these anchor points to position yourself for success.

- *Confession Fire.* Sometimes at our hunting camps we have what we call the "confession fire." Here, you can say whatever is on your mind, without judgment. In this book, I suggest using this section as a journal. I encourage you to answer the questions provided. Each is designed to help you move forward in any area where you may feel a little stuck.

- *Karin's Game Plan.* As a busy working wife and mother, Karin has learned how to prepare the animals we take during the hunt in simple—yet delicious and healthy—ways. This book is filled with low-calorie, health-conscious recipes from Karin and her friends.

1

OLD DAN

We All Have Empty Places

DAVID | Riding a mountain bike through the backcountry of Montana—by myself and before sunrise—had seemed like a good idea at the time. My hunting partner had to work that morning, so this was my first solo elk hunt. On my bike I could slip in undetected, getting farther into the mountains in a fraction of the time. I had no way of knowing what I was about to get myself into. With a heavy miner's light fastened to my head and my pack firmly secured, I started pedaling. Rounding a curve in the road, I dropped down into a cut between two steep cliffs. On the logging road in front of me, I could clearly see the glow of several eyeballs, low to the ground. Thinking they were deer, I quit pedaling and coasted in for a better look.

Now stopped, I could scarcely believe my eyes. I had ridden to within about ten yards of a mountain lion kitten. It was standing in the road, staring at me. Slightly smaller than a yellow Lab, the cat began to pace back and forth. Its long tail flicked from side to side as it seemed to size me up. Shaken, I scanned the area, looking for the rest of those eyeballs. Sure enough, I saw another kitten just up the hill sitting beside a log. My first thought was, *This is so cool!* Then my survival instincts kicked in, spurring my next thought: *Oh no...where's Mom?*

I panned the area, and as I looked to my right, I froze. I had ridden within four yards of her. She stood, staring into my headlamp, obviously confused by what she was seeing. My throat felt like it was filled with sand, and I didn't dare make a move. I had no idea what to do. The only thing I knew about mountain lions came from a book I had read growing up. In the book, the lion killed a hunting dog named Old Dan. Not wanting to share the same fate, I began talking to the cats. "Hello, I'm a human. Go on and leave me alone."

Easton and Karin Holder with "Old" Dan.

The large female cat moved gracefully up the hill to my right, keeping me in her sight. I could see her thigh muscles twitch as I barely dared to breathe. The mother cat and the kitten in the road now joined the kitten perched on the hill above me. I had two choices: I could pass by the three of them and continue the hunt, or I could go back. Keeping my light on them, I forced my shaky legs to move; first one, then the other. I decided to go hunting. I walked past them, pushing my bike. As American actress Dorothy Bernard once said, "Courage is fear that has said its prayers."

Once I got beyond the area where I had encountered the mountain lions, I got on the bike and rode hard for the next 20 minutes. When I finally stopped, my hands were shaking so violently I couldn't undo the buckles on my pack.

After the sun came up and it became light enough to see, I finally got to go elk hunting. In fact, I saw more than 200 of them! Even though I didn't have an opportunity to take a shot that day, I did learn a valuable lesson about being prepared—a lesson I'll never forget.

ON THE HUNT

Karin and I have followed our share of blood trails over the years, from whitetail bucks in Iowa to black bears in Canada. Tracking the red path through timber or across a field of freshly harvested corn never gets old. As hunters, we know the thrill of walking up to the spot where the shot was made, clearly seeing the spray on the ground, and determining the direction the animal went. A well-placed bullet or arrow certainly makes the job easier. Nothing compares to the thrill of tracking your prey.

If the blood is bright red, you probably hit the heart. If it's dark and frothy, the lungs or liver are a better bet. Either way, all your hard work is about to pay off. Not much excites me more than knowing there's a pretty solid chance I'll soon put my hands on the heavy horns of an elk or perhaps run my fingers through the coat of a cinnamon-colored bear. As hunters, we hope for a good trail to follow. Our success depends on it.

The blood trail is connected not only to the kill but also to the time spent planning, preparing, and placing ourselves in a position to quickly and humanely take down the animal. Every blood trail begins long before the shot.

Every hunter has an occasional season when it seems like no matter what we do, we can't connect the arrow to the target. One year our youngest son, Easton, had a season like this. For an adult this can be difficult, but for a kid it's doubly frustrating. Still, it was a good opportunity for me to use this experience as a teaching moment.

Easton had been struggling with arrow placement all season, and while he wasn't ready to quit, he was sick and tired of missing. I'm sure you can relate. We've all had those seasons. Getting the animal in front of you is only half the battle; you still have to make the shot. I kept telling him, "You need to get back on the horse. I don't want to see you give up so easily." It took some doing, but Easton finally agreed to get in the tree stand one more time.

Before too long, his willingness to try again paid off, and a nice buck appeared at 17 yards. This time Easton's arrow found its mark.

As we followed the blood trail through the woods, Easton was worried. At first the streak of red on the leaves was clearly visible, but soon it was barely a trickle.

Easton used the experience to his advantage: "Dad, this is exactly why we need a dog. A dog would help us find this deer." I had heard the pitch many times—not just from Easton but also from Karin and Warren. They were right, but I had my reasons for not getting a dog.

Eventually we found Easton's deer at the bottom of a deep ravine. We hadn't needed a dog to find it, but we sure could have used one to help us drag it back up the hill!

Not every hunt involves killing an animal. Occasionally you find yourself searching for something more. Much more...

There aren't many things my entire family agrees on, but there is one: We all agree the best book ever written is a children's book published in 1961. *Where the Red Fern Grows* tells the story of a boy and his love for two hunting dogs, Little Anne and Old Dan. I don't know if the reason we all love the book so much is that the story is so relatable to our family or if we're like most people and just love dogs. For me, I think it's because the book goes beyond the hunting story and teaches life lessons. Sometimes the hunt isn't about the kill; it's about connecting with those you love, learning lessons along the way, reflecting on the One who created the outdoors for us to enjoy, and seeing how a dog can fill the gaps in our lives.

From mid-December through early April, during deer and shed season, my family found more than one occasion to try to convince me that we needed a dog. Between this and our oldest son, Warren, being about to graduate from high school and head out on his own, things were about to change in the Holder house.

Jeremy Moore is a dog trainer and longtime friend, so when Karin came across his business card one day, my family's dog idea turned into a full-blown plan. Just like Billy in *Where the Red Fern Grows*, Karin and the boys were now on a mission to convince Dad that getting a dog was a good idea.

Every year we hold an archery camp (called Raised at Full Draw) designed to teach kids about hunting. So Karin, being smart and maybe a little bit conniving, had figured out a way to kill a whole bunch of birds with one stone: She would invite Jeremy (who may be one of the best dog trainers on the planet) to camp. Using his dogs, he would help me teach 50 kids about blood trailing and hunting. Jeremy would also have a chance to introduce our camp kids to his training techniques. As Warren says, "Who doesn't love dogs?"

I figured the kids would benefit from interacting with Jeremy's well-trained pack, but knowing my wife, something told me he and his dogs were there for an even bigger reason. Maybe it had something to do with Karin's need to fill the void left by her oldest son moving out. I knew this change would be hard on my wife. Whatever the case, our camp was about to be overrun with dogs.

Sometimes you encounter someone you just can't forget. Jeremy Moore is one of those people. His passion for dog training is so contagious that he convinced me, without much effort, that my family was right. Maybe we were missing something in our lives by not having a dog. When he pulled up to the Raised at Full Draw camp with an eight-week-old black Lab pup in his arms, I knew I was in trouble. Jeremy's passion reminded me of those little things in life that mean so much—little things like owning a dog. One look, and I knew that little pup was our Old Dan.

After camp, the weekly phone calls began. For the next year, I put my trust and my dog in Jeremy's hands. And I waited. In some ways, I related to Billy as the anticipation of our new arrival began to consume my life.

Months passed, and the day finally came. Karin and the boys had no idea they were about to meet Old Dan. My family lives for hunting, so when they needed a distraction for a few hours, all I had to do was offer up some sort of hunt. Anything—from a gator to a grizzly—and my boys are in. That day, they took squirrel hunting to a whole new level as they belly crawled through the brush. Watching them, I just had to shake my head. If our family could take an average day of squirrel hunting and turn it into something this much fun, I could only imagine what they would do when they had a dog to do it with.

When you read *Where the Red Fern Grows*, you know how the story will end, but you can't stop in the middle. The lump starts to build in the deepest part of your throat, and maybe a salty, warm drop runs down your cheek as your heart races with anticipation. You sit on the edge of your seat. You know what's coming, but your emotions are stronger than your determination to stop. I had been sitting on the edge of my seat for months, my emotions barely under control as Jeremy and I were about to give my family one of the greatest gifts of all—the gift of love from a dog.

When Jeremy texted, alerting me to his arrival, I persuaded Karin and the boys to head back to the house. They couldn't understand why I was ready to give up so soon. I'm usually the one who wants to stay out all day. Not today. Today, I was ready to introduce the newest member of our family, Old Dan. Karin, Warren, and Easton stood in the yard as a black bundle of energy jumped off Jeremy's tailgate and ran across the grass to greet them.

It's crazy how this all started—as a book about a young boy and his two dogs with an ending so sad it could make even the toughest man cry. Thankfully for us, this is just the first chapter of our own book, and Old Dan is the newest member of the *Raised Hunting* family.

BEYOND THE HUNT

KARIN | If you've seen David around Old Dan, you're probably wondering why he was ever apprehensive about getting a new dog in the first place. With every good story, there's always a backstory, and that's true for our family as well. Several years before Dan came into our lives, we had a yellow Lab named Arson. We got him when Warren was a baby, and they grew up together, giving Arson a special place in my heart. He was a high-energy dog, and even though he wasn't well trained, we were connected in a way that I can't explain. When I looked at him, he seemed to instinctively know what to do. Dan and I have a similar connection but even more so. If you're a dog lover like I am, I hope you've had a dog like Arson.

Arson was seven months old when he had his first seizure, and it was a big one. Our vet put him on medication, but over the years the seizures only got worse. When he was four years old, we learned that doctors could no longer give him any medications and that it was best to ease his suffering by putting him down. I didn't want Warren or anyone else to be a part of that, so Arson and I took one last car ride together—just the two of us.

I cried nonstop for two weeks. For a long time, I couldn't even think about opening my heart to another dog, even though our home felt empty without one. David resisted the idea of another one not because he didn't love dogs but because he loved me and didn't want to see me go through that pain again.

Old Dan came into our lives at the perfect time, just as my heart was breaking over the fact that Warren would be moving out soon. Of course, Dan could never replace Warren, but he did make the transition easier. As parents, our job is to prepare our kids to leave the nest, but that doesn't mean we're ever fully prepared for it ourselves. I know I wasn't. If you still have children living at home, my advice is to build relationships with them that will continue after they move out. Focus on staying connected and remaining a part of their lives even though you probably won't see them every day. Before we have kids, we focus on what life will be like with them. We don't even consider what life will be like *without* them.

Another issue to deal with when your children leave is your relationship with your spouse. Will your friendship grow? This is why I hunt with David. Hunting is quality time, and I get to see my husband at his absolute best. The man in the tree stand is different from the man on the ground, so I would be missing out on a huge opportunity if I didn't hunt with him. Hunting and spending time together in the outdoors keep us connected. There are many other ways to connect with your spouse as well. The trick is to find what ways work best for you and then do everything possible to take advantage of those opportunities.

DAVID | As hard as it was to see Warren move away from home, we were committed to believing that life isn't empty if God is in it. If you will allow Him in and lean on Him during hard times, emptiness is minimal because He takes up the rest of the space. Even though we all have daily struggles, disappointments, and things we don't always understand, a bigger plan is at work in our lives.

God put each of us here for a purpose, and for whatever reason, I'm pretty good at hunting. That's one of my purposes. Hunting gives me the opportunity not only to follow my passion but also to reach people with a message of hope. When

Karin and David Holder with a slightly older Old Dan.

you recognize that God is on your side and you've been given gifts to give to others, incredible things begin to happen.

We Holders are proof of this. We're a regular family, probably a lot like yours. We sometimes disagree, but because of our relationship with God and love for one another, we always find our way back together. I'd be lying if I said I never struggle with God and why He allows certain things to happen the way they do, but in the end, He and I always come back together.

Perhaps, like me, you've had a lot of pain in your life. When I was 20, my older brother committed suicide, and as I write this chapter, my dad is suffering from Alzheimer's. As a firefighter for 17 years, I can't even begin to explain the heartbreaking things I've experienced firsthand. Some of those memories are still difficult for me at times. Having a relationship with God doesn't take away our pain, but if we accept Him, He always offers a way to work through it.

To be honest, for many years I considered myself a Christian but didn't really include God in my daily life, much less go to church. I just believed He was there, and that was it. The day came when I was out of options and had to turn to something bigger than myself. I thought,

David Holder, what a hypocrite you are. How can you ask God for help when you've always acted like you don't need Him? It was time for me to do more than just wear a cross around my neck. Being a Christian needed to mean something more. Today it does.

Looking back, I don't have many regrets about how Karin and I raised Warren and Easton, but I do regret not taking them to church more often and making God a bigger part of their lives. Even though I can't make it every Sunday, I now include God in my decision-making, and I actively work on my relationship with Him.

If your life feels a little hollow, here's the best advice I can give you: Don't let there be an empty place—God will fill every void in your life, even the void left by one of your children moving out. You just need to let Him in and find a way to connect with Him daily.

It is okay to admit you're human, that you make mistakes, and that you don't always have the answers others are seeking. In fact, this humble honesty is a good thing. God, family, and hunting are the things that fill the holes in my life, and that's where I'm coming from. I would never tell you what to believe, only that you *can* believe.

KARIN | Faith and prayer fill me up just as they fill David. I need them every day. So when I'm feeling empty, I talk to God—usually while I'm taking Dan for a walk. If we had neighbors, they would think I'm a crazy woman. I walk down the road with my dog, talking and shouting—sometimes with my arms flailing all over the place! These are some of my best conversations with God. Meanwhile, Dan just looks at me as if to say, "I know. I know."

When I'm feeling particularly empty, we walk for miles, and Dan is exhausted by the time we get back home. He's by my side every moment, wagging his tail and loving on me when I stop. I believe God uses the dog's love to show me His love. Old Dan is no doubt my best friend!

*May you experience the love of Christ, though it is too great
to understand fully. Then you will be made complete with
all the fullness of life and power that comes from God.*
EPHESIANS 3:19 NLT

ANCHOR POINTS

- A successful hunt is measured not by the size of your kill but by the memories you create while enjoying the outdoors with those you love.
- One of the greatest gifts of all is the gift of love from a dog.
- Build relationships with your kids that will continue after they move out.
- Life is never truly empty if God is in it.

CONFESSION FIRE

Describe your empty places. What will you do about them?

──── KARIN'S GAME PLAN ────

BOONER BURGERS

INGREDIENTS

1½ lbs. ground elk or venison
1 egg white
soy sauce to taste
minced garlic to taste
black pepper to taste

DIRECTIONS

1. Mix all the ingredients together and press into 5 patties.

2. Grill to desired doneness.

NUTRITION

Serving size—about 4.5 oz. (5 servings total)
Calories—181
Fat—3.6 grams
Protein—37.2 grams
Carbohydrates—1 gram

Add a bun, tomato, and avocado if desired.

ROASTED CINNAMON SWEET POTATOES

INGREDIENTS

1 medium-sized sweet potato
Truvia to taste
cinnamon to taste

DIRECTIONS

1. Slice the sweet potato into small cubes.

2. Place on a cookie sheet sprayed with Pam cooking spray.

3. Sprinkle Truvia and cinnamon over the potatoes.

4. Bake at 350 degrees for 40 minutes.

NUTRITION

Calories—114
Fat—.01 grams
Protein—2.1 grams
Carbohydrates—27 grams

2

TIME

Never Give Up

DAVID | A few years ago, while leading an elk hunt in Montana, I learned firsthand just how quickly life can take a drastic turn.

It was early September. The weather was warm, and I was guiding bow hunts for the Rocky Mountain Elk Foundation. There were two groups hunting that day, and sure enough, we spotted some elk heading into a deep canyon. My client wasn't physically able to make the long trek to where we believed the elk would reappear, so the other guide and I decided that he and his client should try to cut them off and get in position for a shot.

As my client and I hung back and watched the two of them head in the direction of the herd, I saw the bull cross and go into a different drainage. My companions were going to the wrong spot, and I had no way to let them know. The bull elk would no doubt pick up their scent, ruining the hunt. I bailed off over the ravine and ran to catch up to them. Once I relayed the message, I started back down the hill and crossed the creek. That's when it happened…

I heard a swooshing sound but didn't see anything. Then I felt a heavy whack on my calf. The snake rattled once before slithering into the bushes. My heart raced, and I started to panic. A rattlesnake bite! I pulled up my pant leg and discovered what I dreaded—there were two tiny puncture marks. I knew I had to get back up the hill while I was able. I stopped every 50 yards or so, trying to maintain my composure. At times I felt nauseated, and at other times I felt fine.

When I finally made it back to my client, he insisted we leave and get the bite checked out. The entire time, I prayed it wouldn't make me sick. Surprisingly, it did not. To be honest, I was just as disappointed about missing the rest of the hunt as I was worried about the bite. Looking back, I probably should have been a little more concerned. A rattlesnake bite is serious, and without proper medical care, it can cause real trouble, real fast.

One thing was for sure: This was one hunt when I was glad Karin wasn't along. I dreaded having to call and tell her. Thankfully, it was a dry bite or the fangs didn't make it far enough through my skin to inject any poison. Whatever the reason, I was grateful. Time was on my side that day.

Time…you can't buy it, but you can spend it. And once it's gone, you can never get it back. Time has a way of showing you what really matters, and the way you use it defines who you are.

Watching the Summer Olympics, I saw a 41-year-old gymnast flip so hard and so fast that I was sure her knees wouldn't support her when she landed. Somehow they did. Then I realized I was watching more than the Olympics—I was watching one of the greatest examples of human dedication, determination, and drive on the planet. But I couldn't help but wonder, *Why do they do it? What drives them to sacrifice their bodies, minds, and all that time with no guarantee of winning a medal?*

What I couldn't have known then was how an elk hunt with my wife and eldest son would help me understand the answer to that "why" question. Now I know that even for an Olympic athlete, it's about more than just the time spent training.

ON THE HUNT

With only three days to hunt, Warren talked me into getting a Montana elk tag. I knew it wouldn't be easy to kill a good bull in such a short amount of time, but I decided to go ahead and spend the money.

Being a successful hunter means battling all kinds of obstacles, especially when hunting elk.

On the first day of the hunt, we saw a few elk entering a drainage that I knew very well. The wind was in our faces, so our chances of remaining undetected were good. If we could get ahead of the elk, we might have an opportunity for a shot. Sure enough, three big bulls (all more than 300 inches) made a brief appearance. But just as we were about to get into position with our bows, a younger spike came in, giving away our position. The bigger bulls skirted just out of bow range.

In all my preseason preparation, I had forgotten to prepare myself for the one constant in elk hunting: God always seems to give elk a fighting chance. Time and time again on the first and second day, we'd be close but just couldn't catch a break with the wind. It was frustrating to once more see two big bulls at less than 100 yards, only to watch them turn and run in the opposite direction. Every experienced elk hunter knows what it's like to have an animal of that size just beyond the distance at which you can safely launch an arrow—seeing those massive horns getting smaller and smaller as the animal gradually slips from sight.

Even though I had spent the summer training and preparing my body for the Montana terrain, I didn't feel like an athlete at all. The long hikes and the short amount of time we had to hunt were already taking their toll on me physically and mentally. By the last day, my patience was wearing thin. With temperatures forecast to be in the nineties, I was less than optimistic. Tomorrow we had to get it done or it wasn't going to happen.

The following morning, with six hours left to hunt, we came in from a different direction. Sitting on the side of a steep hill, we watched a large herd in the canyon just below the skyline. Two decent-sized bulls were fighting, so I felt good about our chances. Calling one of them in would likely be easier, as they were both trying to assert dominance. Once in position, Warren began to cow-call. It wasn't long until one of the bulls stepped out of the brush. Right on schedule, the wind shifted from our faces to our backs. The large bull in front of us raised his head and caught our scent. He whirled around and disappeared.

God seemed to be on their side. Or perhaps He was messing with us. But I wasn't in the mood. Time was running out. Our dedication, determination, and drive were being tested. We now had less than two hours left to hunt, and up to this point, nothing had worked in our favor. We had a choice: We could quit, go home, and accept failure, or we could push forward and hope for one more opportunity.

We chose to keep pushing and give this hunt everything we had. We reached deep, driving our minds and our bodies to the point of total exhaustion, but we still came up empty-handed. As the clock hit zero, signaling it was time to pack up, Karin turned off the camera.

None of us could have predicted what happened next. In our minds, it was time to accept our simple fate. Even with the most valiant effort, we had simply run out of time. As we sat licking our wounds, we heard that subtle snap of a branch cracking.

"Nobody move!" I said under my breath. A bull elk had sneaked up and was standing motionless over my left shoulder at less than 40 yards. With slow movements, Karin attempted to get the camera back on without spooking him. My bow lay on the ground between Warren and me. I glanced at it, knowing I had to get it in my hands. It was now or never.

Somehow, I managed to reach the bow. Slowly, I nocked an arrow.

Incredibly, the bull allowed me to twist, raise, and draw the bow, all while staring at us. Ears twitching, he wasn't going to stay around for long. Now at full draw, I still didn't have a clear shot. The bull began walking—only to stop in the one place where I could take him. I took the shot. It all happened so fast, I wasn't sure where I'd hit him. Warren was pretty sure I had missed. As we sat pondering what had just happened, we heard him crashing in the brush and knew he was down.

At 290 inches, this wasn't the largest elk I've ever killed, but it was certainly the most memorable. What we thought we were going to accomplish in the first ten minutes on the first day we didn't achieve until ten minutes *after* the hunt was over on the last day. Viewers of our television program might not realize that we invest a full five days to acquire every five minutes of footage they see. On *Raised Hunting*, you get to see the victorious end, but you don't see all the times things didn't go as planned. The raw emotion at the end of a successful hunt is only a small part of the outdoor experience. Like you, we've had many missed opportunities.

I entered this elk season asking myself, *Why? Why do we do it? Why do we exhaust ourselves in the pursuit?* As we approached the downed bull, Warren gave the best answer: "It's worth it because it's so rewarding." He was right. The reward is not in winning but in competing. The prize was more than the elk; it was the journey to get there. When you think you've run out of time, just remember what we have learned from past Olympians and from this three-day elk bow hunt. Dig deep. Never give up, because hard work leads us to our greatest moments.

BEYOND THE HUNT

KARIN | David and Warren weren't the only ones feeling the frustration that day. I wanted to give up many times on that hunt. But quitting isn't an option for us. I believe that if you find a way to keep going, you'll get there. Every worthwhile achievement is an uphill climb. I find this is often how God builds faith, character, and courage into my life. The cards were stacked against us: The wind wasn't right, time was running out, and the elk weren't cooperating. Then, in an instant, it all changed—because we didn't give up.

The bull had stood there for 13 minutes, staring us down. I was in an awkward position to be filming, but I knew I couldn't move. Elk are so alert that if you so much as shift your gaze or breathe too hard, they will bust you. As my legs started to tremble, I kept thinking, *I'm not going to be the one to spook this bull.* Out of the corner of my eye, I could see David desperately trying to get to full draw. This was going to happen! David made an incredible shot, and the arrow found its mark. I am in awe of how my husband held it all together in such a critical moment.

Like that hunt, life rarely goes as planned. There are rough patches when nothing seems to be working in your favor. I've learned to trust God during these difficult seasons. Because He has every part of me as a woman, He also has my situation. If you're struggling, step back and stop trying to control everything. Let Him do His work. Get outdoors, shoot your bow, or go for a long walk. Let the fresh air clean out your soul!

DAVID | The things that make for a great hunt also make for a great life. If we had allowed the conditions to dictate whether we hunted that last day, we never would have experienced a positive outcome. Those last seven minutes of the hunt will forever be etched into my brain. To be honest, I can barely even remember the rest of the hunt. It's that one moment that I can't forget—the moment when, in spite of all the setbacks, success was imminent.

You will have great moments in your life as well. Be sure to take the time to stop and recognize them. They usually come after you've been tested. I recently turned 50, and I still have a lot of living left ahead of me. I refuse to allow the difficult things in life to stop me.

Regardless of what you're experiencing, there's a way through it. Refuse to look at your life like a camera snapshot. You're more than the picture in front of you.

On this hunt, we knew we wanted to kill a good bull, but we also knew it was going to be hard. The odds weren't in our favor. But I've always been an underdog—looking for something that has never been done so I can do it for the first time. Call me old fashioned, but I believe with hard work and effort you'll eventually be rewarded. You will be able to accomplish things you never even imagined.

When I worked for the fire department in Montana, I ran an obstacle course—the Firefighter Combat Challenge—as part of my training. It involved running up five stories in less than 12 seconds carrying a 45-pound hose pack and wearing a full complement of firefighter gear. To add to the difficulty, each competitor must breathe through a self-contained breathing apparatus (SCBA). With the gear and the hose pack, you're 95 pounds heavier, and every movement is twice as difficult. Getting to the fifth floor in less than 12 seconds is just the start. The competitor then proceeds through five grueling elements (which include dragging hoses and pounding steel) before reaching the final task: You must "rescue" a 175-pound dummy by dragging it 100 feet to the finish line.

It's physically exhausting, and many firefighters can't complete the entire course on their first try. But the mental anguish is even worse. It's hard to convince the body to do anything when the mind is telling it *No!* With sheer determination and stubbornness, I completed my first attempt in two minutes and twelve seconds, but I wanted to be faster.

The top guys in the world finish in less than 100 seconds. Sounds impossible, right? I thought so too until I met Brad Roe. Brad didn't look like I expected him to; he wasn't the large, muscular guy in a crowd of athletes. I would never have picked him as the fastest firefighter in the world. To my surprise, however, he was. But he didn't start that way.

The first time Brad went through the course, he put himself into renal failure, never making it to the finish line. But here he was now, the top competitor in the world. If he could do it, so could I. In Cheyenne, Wyoming, two years later, I ran the course in 98 seconds.

That's the story of David Holder. I don't always do everything perfectly, but I'm always going to give 150 percent. That's the determined effort I apply to hunting, parenting, my marriage to Karin, and my relationship with God. I ask my boys all the time if they are the kind of person others can count on. Could someone call them at two in the morning to come and pull them out of a mudhole? I strive to be the person who will always be there for others—physically, emotionally, or spiritually.

During this elk hunt, everything was against us, but we still had to be present in that moment. If you're on the verge of quitting, remember why you started in the first place. Simply be willing to show up. You don't have to check off all the boxes or even have a clear plan—just keep going despite the obstacles in front of you. You have no way of knowing how quickly your situation can turn around.

We could have given up the hunt, and no one would have blamed us. All the reasons to quit were easy to see. But this time I put the arrow exactly where I wanted it—not because I'm the best but because I put all my effort into it. Your best is enough!

KARIN | We missed many opportunities on this hunt. In the end, we were successful only because we were willing to *fail forward*. This is something David and I have been learning to do our entire married life.

Several years ago, we found ourselves in northwest Montana, where I was working with Edward Jones and building my financial planning business. David had just retired from the Great Falls Fire Department due to a back injury, so this was a big adjustment for our family.

During this time, we launched *Above the Rest Outdoors*, a regional television show that aired on Root Sports. For us, this program was a prime example of failing forward. The show was nothing special. In fact, it was downright awful! Today, we find it painful to watch. However, out of this perceived failure, we learned what kind of show we *didn't* want to produce. We made major changes as we struggled to create the show we had in our minds, the show that eventually became *Raised Hunting*. We were also grappling with where we lived. The wolves had eaten the deer and elk herd in northwest Montana, so there was no game. We had to travel several hours from home to find game to hunt. As you can imagine, this was extremely difficult to do when we were trying to tell a hunting story.

We finally concluded that we could not continue to live where we were and expect to produce a high-quality hunting show, so we made the difficult decision to move. Now we needed a place to go. Where would that be? We prayed and waited. Finally, we went on a bear hunt in Canada, and on the way home were seriously thinking about moving there. But God had a different plan.

Two days later I received a call from my area leader at Edward Jones, asking if I would consider moving to Winterset, Iowa. Our branch office there had just lost its financial advisor, and they wanted me to fill the spot. We agreed to go check it out.

The moment David and I stepped into the town of Winterset, we both felt that God had placed us there for a reason. I accepted the position, and we moved two months later. Iowa was where we needed to be for our *Raised Hunting* dream to come together. All the struggles and bumps were preparing us for the future God had planned all along.

The time leading up to our move to Iowa taught us what to do and what not to do. The lessons we've learned from our life's journey mirror the lessons we've learned from hunting. Remember, you may not always get the shot you want or bring home the animal you had in mind, but if you learned something in the process, you didn't really fail.

It would have been easy to give up on this elk hunt, and it would have been easy for David and me to give up when our first hunting program looked nothing like what we'd envisioned. We kept moving forward, and we encourage you to keep going as well. Things have a way of turning around fast when you work hard and leave the results to God.

My times are in your hands.
PSALM 31:15

ANCHOR POINTS

- Time has a way of showing you what really matters, and the way you use time defines who you are.
- Hard work leads you to your greatest moments.

- God builds faith, character, and courage into your life during the uphill climb.

- Refuse to look at your life like a camera snapshot. You're more than the picture in front of you.

- Failure is not final if you learned something along the way.

CONFESSION FIRE

When time is running out, dedication, determination, and drive are tested. How are you being tested right now about giving up on something you believe you can achieve? What will you do to keep going?

KARIN'S GAME PLAN

WILD GAME CHILI

INGREDIENTS

2 tsp. olive oil
6 cloves garlic, minced
1 (4 oz.) can sliced mushrooms
1 cup diced green bell pepper
1½ to 2 lbs. ground elk
¼ tsp. black pepper
3 tsp. cumin, or to taste
1½ tsp. chili powder, or to taste
1 (28 oz.) can diced tomatoes, no added sugar
1 (7 oz.) can mild green chilies

DIRECTIONS

1. Heat a large skillet on medium-high heat. Add olive oil, garlic, mushrooms, and green pepper. Stir-fry until lightly browned. Add ground venison (or any wild game).

2. Add the remaining ingredients, turn down heat, and simmer for about 20 minutes.

NUTRITION

Serving size—4.5 oz.
Calories—228
Fat—4 grams
Protein—36.8 grams
Carbohydrates—2 grams

3

HOPE

Overcoming Life's Greatest Obstacles

DAVID | It's easy to move forward when the path is clear. But what about those days when the road in front of you is blocked by an obstacle? What will you do? A few years ago, after moving from the eastern side of Montana to the edge of Glacier National Park, 35 miles south of the Canadian border, I found myself in such a predicament. The road in front of me was blocked. Very blocked.

Karin and I had bought a foreclosed-on log cabin 22 miles from the nearest town. It seemed like the best place on earth to live, but it was very remote—not to mention that the area commonly received between 150 and 300 inches of snow every winter. At times we felt as if we were living at the bottom of a ski slope as the snow kept piling up. It was not an easy place to raise a family, and the predator situation in that part of Montana had gotten out of control. This made it difficult to let the kids play outside. When wolves were reintroduced to the area, their numbers increased rapidly. Our trail cameras were also getting photos of mountain lions right in our driveway. I knew a few grizzly bears lived nearby as well, but I had never seen one.

One afternoon, following a morning when nothing had gone right and Karin and I were at odds, I stormed out of the house to hunt for black bear. For whatever reason, I decided to leave my dirt bike at home and take a four-wheeler instead. I had no way of knowing that decision would save my life. I set out, but when I reached the top of the hill, I decided the weather wasn't safe enough to hunt and started back down the mountain toward home.

The dirt road wound its way through thick woods. As I turned a corner, I could hardly believe my eyes—a big sow grizzly was standing upright in the middle of the road less than 80 yards away! Beneath her were two cubs. One was as big and shaggy as a sheep dog, and the other was a fuzzy little guy. They were not the same size, as if they had been born in different years. As cute as they were, my presence had them on edge, and mom was even more agitated.

The moment she saw me, she hit all fours and raced straight at me. There was no time to back up or turn around, so I did the only thing I could do: I drove straight at her. It was like a game of chicken. She was charging me, and I was speeding toward her, hoping the size of the ATV would intimidate her. Just before we hit, I swerved left and she dove right, dashing off the road and into the thick timber. I thought she was gone, so I kept going. Heart pounding, I looked over my shoulder and was amazed to see that she had come back out of the timber

An angry sow grizzly and her cub—as captured by David Holder's trail cam.

and was now less than ten feet behind me. I hit the throttle and began to pull away, but she kept coming.

I was prepared with both a pistol and bear spray, but I reached instead for my handy-cam. I wanted to prove I was really chased by a grizzly. In my attempt to grab my camera, my thumb kept slipping off the throttle, allowing her to close the distance between us. Finally, I realized if I wanted to survive, I needed to forget about the camera footage and just keep going.

She continued the chase for about 300 more yards before giving up. Once I had put some distance between us, I stopped and looked back. She and her cubs were running up the hill in the opposite direction. It was by far the scariest thing that has ever happened to me while hunting—and the closest I've been to being mauled by a grizzly bear.

By now I was only a quarter of a mile from my house. When I got home, Karin, Warren, and Easton were all out on the front porch. Karin could tell by the look on my face that something was wrong. "What happened?" she asked. I told her about the bear and the lesson I had just learned. Then Karin taught me a lesson.

Remembering the family ordeal we had endured that morning, when no one was getting along, Karin said, "That bear knew how you've been acting, and God was paying you back." She may have said it with a grin, but it woke me up. I'd been squabbling over stuff that didn't matter, when it could have all been over in seconds.

In life there will always be obstacles in the road, and when you encounter them—just as I did with the bear—you must decide what to do. Will you take them on or allow them to consume you? That day, I experienced something terrifying and potentially deadly, but I survived by facing it head-on. That can be your story as well. When the bear charged, so did I. And so can you!

ON THE HUNT

All of us on the *Raised Hunting* team carry one pink arrow in our quiver to promote cancer awareness. Our goal is to get everyone who shoots a bow to do the same. We are passionate about finding a cure for this deadly disease, which strikes seemingly at random and without warning.

Maybe you're like me. No matter how hard I try, I can't imagine being told I have a disease that could take my life. Meeting a grizzly bear on the road is one thing; being diagnosed with cancer is a completely different story. What would I do? Would I fight? Would I blame God? Would my passion for hunting go away?

My best friend, Mitch, and his wife, Tammy, fought this battle. Through their struggle, we at *Raised Hunting* learned a valuable lesson about faith, endurance, and the absolute refusal to give up. This is the story of a battle I never fought.

Mitch and Tammy

It was late whitetail deer season in Iowa, and the weather was perfect. With temperatures forecasted to drop and heavy snow falling, the deer would be on the move. Mitch was already on his way when I called Tammy to see if he had left yet. He had a buck tag burning a hole in his pocket, and I knew just the spot to fill it. When Mitch arrived, I told him he would be hunting spikes and forked horns, but I could tell by his grin he knew otherwise. We had trail camera pictures of several bucks in the 150- to 160-inch range. My goal was to put the buck of a lifetime in front of him.

That evening, Mitch and I were in the deer blind, and I thought I was going to be the teacher. Turns out, Mitch was going to teach me—not about hunting but about life. As we waited in the blind, he started talking about Tammy's struggle. The challenge had been devastating, but the entire ordeal had changed them both for the better.

"After she was diagnosed with breast cancer," he said, "I didn't care as much about the things that didn't matter, and Tammy, as unbelievable as it sounds, became an even better person. Through chemo, the doctors took her to the brink of death to save her life. Those treatments made her so sick, but she fought. I thought more than once she might not make it, but she refused to give up."

His words inspired and challenged me. His perspective on life was so much sharper now. I will be the first to admit I don't always look on the bright side, especially when life puts my family in unexpected situations. I knew it was Mitch's optimism and faith in the Lord that had gotten him through those dark times, but I still felt guilty for not being able to do more. Mitch didn't get his buck on that first hunt, but just listening to him talk, I gained a better understanding of the life-and-death struggle Tammy had been through. And she had survived.

The second evening, we were back in the blind. By now we had seen more than 50 deer, including some really nice bucks that were too young to shoot. I hoped a certain deer would make an appearance—a deer I was obsessed with. I call him the Big Eight.

A group of does were feeding on the ridge in front of us. They kept looking nervously to the right, spooked. I could tell something was coming. Could it be the Big Eight or something even bigger? "Big buck, big buck," Mitch chanted under his breath.

I turned to see a true Iowa giant heading straight to the blind. Mitch's breath was so heavy and loud in my earphones that I had to take them out of my ears. Watching as the buck drew nearer, Mitch asked me if this was a "shooter." I could feel his tension and excitement when I told him to go for it.

The buck stopped broadside at 50 yards. Mitch took a deep breath and squeezed the trigger of his muzzleloader. A perfect shot.

As we approached the downed buck, I could see his antlers sticking out of the brush. It wasn't the Big Eight—it was a big ten! We had seen this buck on trail cameras but had no idea he was even in the area. To top it off, I had always severely underscored his rack due to the size of his enormous body. This was a true Boone and Crockett deer, measuring 175 inches. When we walked up to him, I knew this was a special buck that God had blessed us with, and no one deserved him more than my best friend.

As Mitch sat down in the snow beside the deer of a lifetime, all he could do was thank me for this day and thank his wife for inspiring him. When the reality set in of what he had just done and the journey it took to get there, he began to cry. I expected nothing less from him. Mitch is the kind of guy you can call when you're having a bad day, and he will make you feel better. He's truly a good man and a constant reminder that life is about more than just hunting. The joy of killing his best buck in no way compares to the joy of having a healthy wife. Tammy battled breast cancer and won. Her message is hope.

KARIN | David and Mitch have been friends since the early 1990s, when they were both firefighters. The bond between them is from God, no doubt. This hunt was special to all of us, but David was especially excited to have this hunt with his friend, who had endured so much. David and I have spent many years raising our family and focusing on our careers. We tended to be a bit self-centered. Now it was time to give back, to share what we had with someone else. God delivered in a huge way with Mitch's harvesting of the largest deer our family had ever laid eyes on.

Unfortunately, breast cancer has affected most of us in one way or another. At *Raised Hunting,* we believe we need to act, not just sit back and watch this terrible disease continue to affect the people we love. We invite you to join us in carrying one pink arrow as a reminder of the battle many women fight daily. We sell pink arrow wraps and donate the proceeds to breast cancer research. To order your own pink arrow wraps, visit us online at www.raisedhunting.com.

BEYOND THE HUNT

DAVID | Mitch and Tammy offer a perfect example of what you should do when life throws you a curveball. Instead of giving up, they decided to rise up and face what was in front of them. As you grow older, you realize that life is a series of obstacles. After you overcome one, you will soon face another. Life is not easy, but God never promised it would be. Don't fall into the trap of believing that if you do all the right things, God will make life simple. That couldn't be further from the truth. If you buy into that mindset, you'll always be frustrated or disappointed.

If I've learned anything in my half century on this earth, it's that I grow most as a person when I'm faced with a challenge. Sometimes the challenges are small potatoes—a food plot that didn't come up, a deer you couldn't shoot because the camera angle was off, or a neighbor who killed the buck you've had your eye on for a few years. Other times, as was the case with Tammy, the challenges are huge, and you feel as if you're staring at a problem the size of a mountain. Whether the things that block your path are big or small, you must face them with the same amount of intensity. Full speed ahead!

Most of us pray when things aren't working in our favor. God has our full attention when we're hurting, enduring a family crisis, or struggling with a health issue. We often look to Him when we can't figure things out on our own. But how much better it is to include Him in the first place, to be thankful to Him for all things on normal days when we aren't falling apart.

I'm slowly learning that what I sometimes see as an obstacle is really a stepping-stone. God is usually trying to take me to the next level of success in life. No matter what is in front of me, I can use it as the very thing that moves me on to whatever God has in store for my future.

Regardless of what you've been through, there is hope. There are still good things to come, and your best days can still be ahead of you. You can trust God with the future, and you can follow Tammy's example by not only surviving your challenge but using it to make you into an even better person. Don't waste your pain. Use it!

KARIN | Life is full of obstacles, and though I've never had cancer, I do know what it is like to feel completely overwhelmed. Challenges make up our life experience and determine who we are. I've learned that obstacles are temporary and short-term issues—and even if they seem long-term, they're still temporary because this world is not our home.

You're on a path that leads to the future even if you have no idea where it's going. There will always be roadblocks, caution lights, and forks in the road. You will have to make hard choices to follow the right path. I've always relied on two things to help me make this decision.

First is my faith. I believe life's greatest obstacles will work out in God's time and for God's purpose. I practice letting go. In the case of something out of my control, such as an illness or accident, turning it over and trusting in God is my only choice. I know no other way.

Second is my value system. What are my values, and is the path I'm about to take aligned with them? Many times, I have taken a path that was not aligned with my values and certainly not aligned with God's. In those instances, I found my life spiraling out of control. I didn't like the feeling of being disconnected from God and making choices that were not influenced by Him.

I have fallen to my knees and had serious talks with God about myself. I've been forced to consider my behavior and my daily actions—and how they were affecting the people around me. Sometimes we think the choices we make affect only ourselves. But in fact, the ripple effect can be huge. Were those actions serving me well and helping me make progress, or were they leading me down a dead-end road? Sometimes I must shift back down into first gear, list my values (God, family, health, career, personal growth and development), and align my daily actions with those values. Then I must repeat the process until the journey is complete.

If an obstacle on your life's road has caused you to give up hope, my best advice is to keep going. Keep putting one foot in front of the other. Talk to God even when you don't want to. Eventually you'll find your way out of depression and loss. Every day is a new day, a new opportunity, and a new chance. Many instances in my life, I've felt beaten down, lost all hope, and thought, *What's the point?* Then something inside me snaps! I refuse to let it beat me. Maybe I'm just stubborn, but I've learned to fight back. I stop the negative self-talk. I turn to those I trust for advice, prayer, and friendship that will lift me up and improve the situation. It's not easy, but if I can do it, so can you.

DAVID | I've stared at a lot of mountains in my life, both physically while hunting and metaphorically while hurting. I remember standing in Montana, looking at the mountains for the first time and saying to myself, *Nobody can climb those. It's impossible. They're too steep.* Or were they? Later, after getting in top condition for the Firefighter Combat Challenge, I climbed those same mountains—with an elk strapped to my back. The obstacle was not the mountain, but what I believed about the mountain.

Karin and I have a normal marriage. We're just regular people. We don't always agree on everything, but in the end, we find a way to make it work. However, it hasn't always been that way. We've had our mountains to climb. There have been major obstacles, especially early in our marriage. If you've seen us work together on *Raised Hunting*, this might come as a surprise to you, but there was a time when I didn't think we were going to make it (and she didn't think so either).

At the time, Warren was very small, and Easton hadn't been born yet. During this difficult period, we considered calling it quits. I remember driving down the road, feeling hopeless and wondering what would become of us. A Zac Brown song came on the radio. I can't remember the title, but he was singing about family and picking up his son. Tears filled my eyes, and I had to pull over. I sat at the side of the road crying because I realized that Karin and I weren't the only ones involved here.

Those mountains I had looked at in Montana and believed were impossible to climb? They now seemed small compared to the mountain Karin and I were facing in our marriage. It was difficult for me to move past my pride and admit I was a part of the problem. I had trained myself to climb mountains, but I didn't have a workout regimen to fix my marriage. I think most married people get to that place at some point. Maybe not to the extreme Karin and I did, but we all face major obstacles.

I knew I had to change if we were going to stay married, but I didn't know where to turn or what to do. We needed help. For years, Karin had tried to get me to go to church with her, but I just never felt comfortable there. Don't get me wrong; I believed in God and talked to Him on occasion, but I had no desire to go to church. Yet, although I was living my dream in Montana, my life was a disaster. I had the job

I wanted, a three-year-old son, and a beautiful wife. But even with all that, I was a mess.

I drove home that day and asked Karin if she would consider finding a church that we both agreed on. Fortunately, she said yes. This was a turning point for us. For the first time, we sat down and discussed our need for someone to help and guide us. I didn't need a hunting guide. I needed someone to help me with my life. Karin opened the yellow pages and chose a church in Great Falls, Montana. She called and talked to the pastor, Dennis Reece. After their conversation, she was convinced this was the right church. With nothing to lose, I agreed to give it a shot, and we attended a service the following Sunday. For the first time in my life, I felt comfortable going to church—like I was supposed to be there. Maybe it was the timing, but I think it was more about the people and how they welcomed us.

The church scene was a new experience, but just being there made me realize I didn't have to move life's obstacles by myself. God would help me if I trusted Him. At first it was a little scary because I was accustomed to being the guy who did life my own way. I believed I could take care of anything. Having to give up my arrogance and completely surrender to God wasn't easy, but it was the best decision I've ever made.

That was more than 20 years ago. Now I wonder what would have happened if I hadn't heard that song, walked into the church, and given my life to God. Where would I be today? I certainly wouldn't be telling stories about a family who hunts together. I wouldn't be sharing the outdoors with Karin or writing this book for you. Thank you, Zac Brown. Thank you, Dennis Reece. Most importantly, thank You, God, for reaching out to me that day, because fixing my marriage was the biggest mountain I've ever climbed.

KARIN | Though I've never been in Tammy's situation, I have been in Mitch's position regarding David's health. My husband has always been both physically and mentally strong. He puts the needs of others ahead of his own, which is one of the reasons he flourished at the fire department. Like any firefighter's spouse, I always worried about his safety; however, I knew he loved what he was doing, so I did my best to support his decisions. The wear and tear of being a fireman affected his body over the years. It was beginning to make it difficult for him to do his job at the level he expected from himself.

In 2008, while on a call, David severely injured his back. This time, he was out of commission, unable to do anything and in a tremendous amount of pain. We spent week after week, month after month, visiting doctors and surgeons, trying to find a way to repair his body so he could return to work. The doctors told us David had the back of an 80-year-old man. And he was only 39! Finally, the surgeons suggested a spinal fusion. I didn't know what that meant at the time, but David did. The surgery would take away the pain, but it would also limit his mobility and destroy any hope he had of returning to work. There was no way my husband was going to do that. Our situation was going from bad to worse, and the answers we were getting were not the answers we wanted or believed God had for us.

Our lifestyle has always has been active. We have climbed mountains, exercised, and hunted. At the time, his diagnosis sounded to us like that lifestyle was at an end. As a wife, my main concern was that my husband get relief from his pain, but I was also terrified of what this would do to him.

We had an enormous, life-altering decision to make and not much time to make it. In addition, I was busy building my career at Edward Jones Financial and raising the boys.

Finally, after a year and a half, David decided not to have the surgery but to manage the pain as best he could. This meant he would have to alter just about everything in his life, including hunting. He would have to ask others for help, which no one in our family is good at doing. No longer would David be the one to pack out the elk. That role now shifted to friends, Warren, Easton, and me. The look of devastation in his eyes was heart wrenching. I had to remind him he could still go and participate in the hunt—just without the heavy lifting. To make matters worse, David could not return to the fire department. He was urged to take an early retirement. In 2009, he retired from the Great Falls Fire and Rescue as a captain.

Now we had a choice—sit and sulk or find another route. We decided to find another path up life's mountain.

Today, most people don't even know about David's back injury. They look at him and think he seems fine, though he still struggles sometimes. If it weren't for an episode of *Raised Hunting* called "The Bond," few would know about his firefighting days and the toll they took on his body.

While leaving his career was difficult on all of us, it did open the door for us to begin our journey on outdoor television. But that's a different story...

> "I know the plans I have for you," says the LORD. "They are plans for good and not for disaster, to give you a future and a hope."
> **JEREMIAH 29:11 NLT**

ANCHOR POINTS

- When challenged by an unexpected obstacle, move confidently forward, trusting God with the outcome.
- Life is more than just hunting.
- Instead of giving up, rise up.
- Every day is a new day, a new opportunity, and a new chance.
- Obstacles become stepping-stones when used for personal growth.

CONFESSION FIRE

Life is too precious to waste. Describe what you believe to be your greatest obstacle. How will you get around it? What will you do differently?

KARIN'S GAME PLAN

ALYSSA'S ELKCHILADAS

INGREDIENTS

2 lbs. ground elk

1 (8 oz.) container light cream cheese (Fat-free cream cheese works as well, but be aware that it tends to stick a little more to the bottom of the pan and doesn't look as creamy. But it melts into the ground meat just the same.)

1 (28 oz.) can green enchilada sauce

1 (4.5 oz.) can diced green chilies, drained (optional)

10 whole wheat (and low-carb) 6-inch (fajita size) flour tortillas

1 (7 oz.) bag fat-free mozzarella cheese

DIRECTIONS

1. Preheat the oven to 400 degrees.

2. Cook the ground elk in a skillet and drain off any excess fat. Don't rinse the meat; you want the meat to remain warm.

3. While keeping the skillet on low heat, add the cream cheese, 1 cup of enchilada sauce, and optional green chilies. Continue stirring until the cream cheese is melted. Turn the heat off.

4. Spray a 9 × 13-inch baking pan with nonstick spray and pour enough green chili sauce to lightly cover the bottom of the pan.

5. Spoon the meat mixture evenly onto 10 whole wheat tortillas, roll up the tortillas, and place in the baking pan.

6. Pour the remaining enchilada sauce over the enchiladas in the pan and top with fat-free mozzarella cheese.

7. Bake at 400 degrees for 18 to 25 minutes or until cheese browns and enchilada sauce boils around the edges. You may have to cover with tinfoil for the remaining 5 minutes if the cheese browns before the enchilada sauce begins to boil.

NUTRITION

Serving size—2 enchiladas (5 total servings)
Calories—547
Fat—14.6 grams
Protein—63.4 grams
Carbohydrates—39 grams

4

LOST

Understanding Your Purpose

DAVID | We live in a world that's changing faster than most people can keep up with. We can find anyone, anywhere, anytime with just a few clicks of the keyboard. However, most of us can't even find ourselves, let alone discover why God placed us here. We've come to rely on self-help books, cell phones, and apps for motivation, entertainment, and inspiration. To me, it seems like we no longer have time to solve even the simplest of problems on our own. And why should we? We can google it.

When you depend on others more than you depend on yourself, it's easy to lose your way. The only thing worse would be to stop depending on God for guidance and His help to discover your purpose.

Your purpose is God's gift to you. What you do with it can be your gift to Him.

From as early as I can remember, spending time in the outdoors has always stirred something inside me. Growing up in Virginia, I looked for every opportunity to go hunting. My family hunted, but they didn't take it to the extreme I was looking for. I had to learn a lot about hunting on my own, and I figured it out early in life.

I'm guessing that's one of the reasons I'm so passionate about our Raised at Full Draw hunting camps. I receive an incredible amount of satisfaction from teaching the next generation of hunters the things I had to learn the hard way. Even if you can't make it to one of our camps, you can make that same investment by passing on the lessons you've learned about hunting and the outdoors to the youngsters around you.

When I was ten, I went on a deer hunt I will never forget. The plan was simple enough: A group of us were going to walk through the woods to a power line and (we hoped) jump a deer along the way. When I reached the power line, someone was supposed to be 100 yards to my left and someone else 100 yards to my right. But when I arrived at the power line, they weren't there. Waiting at least 20 minutes without hearing or seeing a soul, I began to get scared.

Deciding they must have gone farther without telling me, I continued on and ended up in a deep ravine. There was still no sign of anyone, and it was starting to get dark. Panic set in. I let out a series of yells. When no one answered, I turned around and started back toward the road, but I wasn't sure about the route. Tears were streaming down my face, but I knew I couldn't just sit and wait for someone to figure out I was missing. *Go straight, David,* I told myself. *Just go straight and you'll make it out.*

Eventually, I did make it back to the road. I emerged only about 200 yards from the truck. Wiping the tears from my eyes, I saw my friends all standing there. I pretended everything was fine because I didn't want anyone to know how terrified I had been just a few minutes before. I learned a valuable lesson that day: You can be panicked and be finding your way *at the same time.* You may feel lost, but that doesn't necessarily mean you are.

It's one thing to be lost in the woods; it's another to feel so lost in life that you don't know where the road is. Technology can locate you and help you make it out of even the most rugged terrain, but a GPS is useless when it comes to the important things, like understanding your purpose—the reason God put you here in the first place.

Life, like hunting, involves a series of choices. The right choices eventually lead to success. The wrong ones keep you trapped in failure and frustration. Maybe you are caught up in some bad choices right now, and you recognize what I'm saying is true. It's never too late to turn it around. Especially if God helps you do it.

I'm not saying it's easy to find your place in this world. But I am saying you can do it, and when you do, you'll know it. The most important thing is that you don't give up, even if you feel lost. Just keep going.

Bowhunting from a tree stand, Easton Holder harvested a buck and a doe on the same day.

ON THE HUNT

At my age, I'm beginning to realize that I'm caught somewhere between a rotary phone and an iPhone. I still remember when hunters relied more on skill, persistence, patience, and good old-fashioned hard work—and less upon the latest gadget. I believe hunting was much less complicated before we depended so heavily on technology. Warren and Easton, however, learned to hunt using technology to locate trail cameras, check wind direction, and map their way to and from the deer stand. So maybe old-school guys like me and young up-and-comers like my boys can learn from one another. Our styles may sometimes clash, but our purpose remains the same.

Early one bow season in Iowa, Karin and I were hunting whitetail deer. Warren and Easton were also hunting together, not far from us. Karin spotted a doe by the fence line. "I can just see her legs," she whispered. "She's walking to the right." We watched the doe take the trail leading past our stand, but she stopped in one of the only places where Karin didn't have a clear shot.

One of our goals is to treat every animal with the respect it deserves. That means we do everything in our power to harvest whatever we are hunting as humanely and ethically as possible. Without a good shot, Karin allowed the doe to walk by. Once the deer was out of sight, I took out my phone to text the boys.

"Seeing if you boys are good. Did you get into the stand okay?"

"Yeah, we're good," Easton replied.

Karin looked at me and grinned. "What are you doing?"

"Texting the boys."

"You're always giving them grief about texting and being on their phones, and now you're doing it!"

Karin was partially right. I did give Warren and Easton a hard time about messing with their phones when they were supposed to be concentrating on the hunt. I wanted them to focus on what they were doing.

Deer movement that morning was slow for us. For the boys, it was a different story. I received a text from Warren: Easton had shot a doe and then a buck, but he thought the second shot might have been a little high. They were going to look at the footage they'd acquired and then decide how to proceed with finding the buck.

I pressed for more details. I knew the stand they were hunting from was quite a few feet off the ground. Even if the arrow placement had been high, the angle should have been steep enough to make a clean kill. When bowhunting from a tree stand, the exit wound will be lower than the entry point of the arrow. When the animal is below you, hitting a little high isn't necessarily bad. In fact, it could be exactly what you want.

Finally, in his effort to give me the information I was insisting on, Warren texted me a trail camera photo of a buck, marking the spot where he believed the arrow had passed through the buck Easton shot. Twenty years ago, it would have been impossible to send a photo like this to someone else's phone, let alone draw a red dot on it, showing the exact spot where the arrow penetrated the animal. Still, there was no way to know for sure until we looked at the camera footage. All the technology in the world couldn't answer my questions. Maybe the deer was lost. Maybe it wasn't. All we could do was climb down, go home, and wait.

Back at the house, Easton opened his laptop and loaded the camera footage. With his finger tracing the computer screen, he said, "This one is him. I shot him thinking he was 25 yards, but he was only at 20." We played the footage at regular speed and then in slow motion. That's when I saw it. "Do you see that? That's him going down!"

They'd recorded the deer falling and didn't even know it. I was confident we could find the buck, but there was only one way to know for sure: We had to go back to the spot from which Easton had shot and go from there. So off we went. Before we could even get to the blood trail, Warren spotted the buck lying just a few yards away. The shot was good, and the camera footage had been spot-on. The buck had gone down exactly where I thought he had. It was the biggest buck Easton had ever killed (148 inches), and he had also killed his first doe that same day.

This hunt proves technology can help you kill a big deer by finding the right place, tree, and trail...but that, when it comes down to it, you still have to make the shot. You can love it or hate it, but technology has a purpose. As the old man in our family, I'm trying to embrace it.

BEYOND THE HUNT

Understanding the need for the newest gadget while hunting is one thing; understanding your purpose and why God put you here is another. When I'm feeling a little lost and struggling to know which way to go, I follow a four-step process:

1. Do I need to reevaluate? Sometimes you just need to change what you're doing. As the common saying goes, insanity is doing the same thing over and over again and expecting different results. When your life doesn't feel very purposeful, it could be time for a significant change.

I've never forgotten a piece of advice my father passed on to me when I was growing up: If you're doing something for others and your intentions are good, then you're doing what is right. Even if what you did or said wasn't that helpful to someone else, if you weren't being malicious and thought it was going to help, you're okay.

If your life feels empty of purpose, reevaluate your intentions.

2. Is there another way to achieve my goal? If your life is not working, try another route. Recognizing what God has laid out for you is not the same as following it. The path to your goal might be different from the one you originally imagined.

By now, you probably realize how strongly I believe a successful life can parallel a successful hunt. Sometimes while hunting, I have to change how I approach an animal. If the wind is at my back, the animal is likely to pick up my scent. To increase my chance of success, I might need to circle around so the wind is blowing in my face. In life and in hunting, there is often a more successful path. When you find that path, be sure you take it.

3. Have I already accomplished more than I thought? For example, if your goal is to run a marathon but you only run a half marathon, did you really fail? It's better to shoot for the moon and get halfway there than to shoot for the ceiling and make it. Anytime you're doing something you've never done, life feels more purposeful—even if you didn't quite get to where you wanted to go.

Hunting can be that way. The goal might be to kill a huge elk or your biggest buck, but that doesn't happen every time. Maybe instead of being disappointed, you should look at what you accomplished. Perhaps you walked into the woods in the dark and found your way back using only a compass. That's a huge accomplishment! Refuse to get lost in the result. Instead, enjoy the journey you're taking to get there. Chances are you're accomplishing more than you think.

4. Is this impossible? Years ago, I lifted extremely heavy weights. I didn't do it because I wanted the biggest biceps. I did it because I wanted to be the guy at the fire department others could count on to move even the heaviest objects. I lifted to be strong—period. My goal was to weigh 200 pounds and bench press 405. I was eventually able to bench press 400 pounds multiple times, but I could not add 5 more pounds. I never did reach that goal.

Things changed for me when I started running obstacle courses. I cut about 15 pounds and lost some muscle mass. However, I was in the best shape of my life and felt far better than when I was super strong. Even though my goal at the time was to bench 405, I found out I didn't need to reach that goal to be at my physical best. Warren often asked me, "Don't you wish you had gotten 405 at least once?" I'd just shrug and shake my head no. It doesn't matter to me.

When life feels impossible, I believe it's because God has something out there that is far better for you. If you are fixed on a goal and refuse to entertain the idea that perhaps God has a different path for you, you can easily lose all sense of purpose.

The hardest thing for any archer to do is to let down his or her bow after getting to full draw because the shot isn't good. But when your view of the animal is obstructed, letting down is often the only choice. Similarly, you will have times in your life when you think there's only one shot and you have to take it. However, I've learned you don't have to take every shot. There will always be another. You need to choose the right shots.

KARIN | Unfortunately, a lot of people feel lost. They wander around, reacting to the demands of life, spending day after day going through the motions and getting caught up in a whirlwind of activity that in the end really doesn't mean anything. I know this because there were days that I, too, went through the motions. I would get up, take the kids to school, go to work, fix dinner, do laundry, straighten up the house, and go to bed. Then I'd get up the next day and do it all over again. I was frustrated, angry, and disappointed in life, with a massive empty feeling that went way down in my soul. But I didn't stay in that condition, and you don't have to either.

I discovered that the way out of frustration was to focus on those things that truly mattered to me. As you probably know by now, my husband and boys top that list. I figured out that I had to let go of some of the temporary things that were filling up my day without producing anything of lasting value. Though there are still responsibilities that must be accomplished, I've pared down my life to what matters most, the things that bring me the fulfillment and joy God intends. For me, that was easy—spending time with family doing what we love and feel called to do.

Finding your purpose in life is like finding your destination on a family vacation or trip—only on a much larger scale. God's ultimate purpose gives you direction and a reason for going in the first place. You seldom arrive anywhere by accident. So I guess the million-dollar question is this: How do you find your purpose? Many people have no idea where to even begin when trying to answer this question. I think it's because getting an accurate answer requires that we dig down and honestly assess the condition of our lives.

We discuss this in my leadership workshop. My students answer the following questions: What makes you happy? What do you dream about? What do you cry about? What do you sing about? What are you doing when you feel peaceful and content?

In today's world of technology, we're so used to relying on our phones and computers for information that we've stopped looking into our hearts and souls for answers. Siri can't tell me what my purpose is, no matter how many ways I ask her. The same is true for you. Siri doesn't know your purpose. Your friends don't know, your spouse doesn't know, and your pastor doesn't know. Only you can discover your purpose, and that takes courage.

DAVID | Karin and I have learned that when we pursue God's purpose, our dreams can be realized in ways we weren't expecting, and it's our relationship with the Creator that gives rise to our greatest opportunities. He moves us in the direction we're supposed to go. I used to believe I found my purpose on accident, but I now understand that even though I didn't always know what I was ultimately designed to do and be, God did. He has been preparing me my entire life for something I had no idea was coming.

Through *Raised Hunting*, we are impacting hundreds of thousands of lives each week. That is our purpose, but it didn't start that way. We get calls and letters all the time from people we've never met, telling us how we've helped save their marriage or pulled them through the loss of a loved one. Honestly, my goal in creating the television show was to help save hunting. God had a different purpose in mind. As viewers began to take note of who I am as a husband and father, who Karin is as a wife and mother, and of our faith, many found the answers they were looking for in their own lives. Again, I had no idea this was going to be a by-product of the television show, but God did.

You don't have to be a preacher to impact those around you for God. You can make a difference in your ordinary, everyday life. As a matter of fact, I believe that's God's plan for most of His people—to positively affect those around in an authentic, organic way. God can certainly use you the way He is using *Raised Hunting*. This happens when your purpose and His purpose collide and become interwoven.

I was a firefighter and am now hosting a hunting show on one of the largest outdoor networks. Who knows where I'll be or what I'll be doing in five years? I do know, however, that if I keep my relationship with God first, where I'm going will be more meaningful than where I've been.

I used to think I had to know every detail of the future and exactly where the path was leading. Now I just go along with whatever God has in store for me. I thank God every day for what I have and what I'm doing. Don't get me wrong—I still occasionally argue with God over how my life is going, but I've learned to trust Him even when I don't always understand, realizing that what is happening today is moving me closer to where He wants me to be tomorrow.

If you're still struggling to find your purpose, know that God is patient. He has waited a long time for me to recognize how He's been leading me, and He is patient with you too. Regardless of who you are or how old you are, God is with you, ready for you to respond. You just have to let Him in.

KARIN | I've had many conversations over the years with God about what my purpose is. I've asked more than once, "What do You want me to do?" I've figured out that if God wants me to go in a certain direction, He'll allow things to happen so that I can get there. I'm not saying He perfectly marks the road so I'll know every twist and turn, or that everything is easy. In fact, it's often just the opposite. But if I'm on the right path, God will help me get there. I've also found that God has *many* purposes for us, and His purposes are likely to change over time as we grow in our relationship with Him and with ourselves. Here's an example.

Right now, one of my purposes is to help women understand their value. I want to partner with them to build their confidence and empower them to be all God created them to be. This hasn't come easy. Before I could do this, I had to first learn my own value. If I wanted to empower others, I had to empower myself because I can't give away what I don't have. After years of walking and talking with God about my own identity, I've concluded that I'm His dearly loved child, teeming with potential and created in His image. With this revelation, I'm equipped to help other women walk in this truth. Conveying this truth is now one of my main purposes, but only because I prepared myself to walk in it.

How did I identify my value, and why did I not understand it earlier? Why did I have low self-worth and low self-esteem? Like you, I have dealt with many of life's hurts—some caused by my own choices and some caused by other people. One of mine was a product of the generation in which I was raised.

I knew my father loved me. But even though he found time to attend my brother's life events, he never attended my two sisters' or mine. My mom was committed to attending everything, but Dad's absence sent a strong, unspoken message: "You're not important."

Our heavenly Father tells me that I am important and that He loves me. I have come to realize that what people of this world say to me or think of me does not matter. What God's Word says about me is what is true. If someone is telling you that you're not good enough, skinny enough, pretty enough, or smart enough (and you believe it), I challenge you to compare that to what the Bible says about you.

*It's in Christ that we find out who
we are and what we are living for.*
EPHESIANS 1:11 MSG

ANCHOR POINTS

- Your purpose is God's gift to you; what you do with it can be your gift to Him.

- You can be panicked and be finding your way at the same time.

- In life and in hunting, there is always a more successful path. Find that path and take it.

- It's better to shoot for the moon and only get halfway than to shoot for the ceiling and make it.

- Your relationship with the Creator gives rise to your greatest opportunities.

- When life doesn't feel very purposeful, it could be time for a significant change.

CONFESSION FIRE

Finding your purpose is often tied to asking yourself questions like these: What makes me happy? What do I dream about? What do I cry about? What do I sing about? What am I doing when I feel at peace and content?

KARIN'S GAME PLAN

ELK LOIN STIR-FRY

INGREDIENTS

1 cup brown rice
1 lb. elk steak or backstrap
2 red peppers (sliced)
2 green peppers (sliced)
2 cups broccoli florets
1 cup mushrooms
stir-fry sauce

DIRECTIONS

1. In a rice cooker, cook rice in 2 cups of water.

2. Spray an electric skillet with a nonstick cooking spray. Slice the elk into thin strips and cook until desired doneness.

3. Remove the meat from the skillet and add to the skillet sliced peppers, broccoli, mushrooms, or any veggies you desire. Cook 3 to 5 minutes, being careful not to overcook.

4. Place the elk meat back into the skillet with the vegetables and add any stir-fry sauce. I use a low-sodium sauce from the supermarket.

5. Stir the meat and vegetables together until they are evenly coated.

6. Plate the rice first and then add the meat and vegetables.

I always cook up extra so that we can have it on hand as a go-to meal.

NUTRITION

Calories—215
Fat—3.7 grams
Protein—29.2 grams
Carbohydrates—18.1 grams

FEAR

Turn Your Fears into Focus

KARIN | After David retired from the fire department in September 2009, we moved to Olney, Montana, and lived there until the spring of 2012. Olney is only 30 miles from the Canadian border in the northwest corner of the state, nestled by the Stillwater River in the Flathead Forest. To the north is the Whitefish Mountain Range, home to one of the largest concentrations of grizzly bears in North America. At one time, Olney was a booming sawmill town, but it became more like a ghost town after the price of timber dropped. By the time we arrived, Olney had a whopping population of twenty. Twenty-four, if you counted the Holders.

We moved to Olney because my firm asked if I would take over a nearby office that had just lost its financial advisor to another company. I accepted the offer, thinking it was a good career move. And with David retiring from the fire department, nothing was keeping us in Great Falls. We thought it would be a good way to start a new journey.

It didn't take long to find a beautiful log home in the middle of the forest. It had been foreclosed on during the financial crisis in 2008. Buying it was exciting. Keeping it up? Not so much, as this type of home requires a lot of maintenance. Still, it was the first piece of land

The Holder cabin in Olney, MT. Ten acres surrounded by grizzly bears, wolves, and mountain lions.

we ever owned. Ten acres surrounded by grizzly bears, wolves, and mountain lions! What's not to love?

Imagine walking on your own land, maybe out shooting your bow, and constantly having to look over your shoulder to make sure nothing is hunting you. That was the environment we lived in. I was terrified to let Warren and Easton, ages twelve and eight, go fishing or do anything outside. But I knew I couldn't keep them inside all the time. That was no life for a couple of rowdy boys. David and I needed to teach them to adapt and get smart about how to handle themselves in potentially dangerous situations. This included teaching them things like intentionally making noise when they went outside to let the critters know they were there.

One day David was out of town on a trip, and the boys and I were home. With the snow and rain falling nonstop, we had been cooped up for a long time. The boys were about to drive me nuts. Before I blew a cork, I sent them outside to pick up sticks in the yard. Suddenly, they came bursting through the front door yelling, "Mom, come out here! You have to see this!" When I joined them, both were excited but shaken. Wondering what could be wrong, I started asking questions.

The boys had seen mountain lion tracks and telltale signs that the animal had killed a deer right in our backyard. It had been raining for three days, and had only stopped a few hours before I'd sent them outside. The tracks had to be fresh.

Fear twisted my gut, but with mama bear determination, I loaded two 12-gauge shotguns—one for me and one for Warren. Easton ran the video camera. With me leading, we went outside to the place of the kill, which was about 30 yards from the back deck. Sure enough, deer hair was all around, as well as huge drag marks with cat claws straddling the trail. The lion had dragged the deer on a route passing only 15 yards from the front door. We were scared because we knew this dangerous predator was way too close for comfort, but all I could think about was getting this cat off our property.

Blood, hair, and lion tracks pointed the way. Sweating, hair raised, and hearts pounding out of our chests, we inched forward. We hadn't gone far when we found a pile of deer remains. The fresh kill was chilling proof that the lion had hunted in our backyard just a few minutes before Warren and Easton had gone outside. We didn't ever see the lion that day, but the photos we discovered from the trail cameras were sobering reminders of just how closely we were living with wild animals.

Life can be scary and supercharged with emotion. I was glad we didn't run into the lion that day, but I was also fascinated by the course nature takes and the raw, wild experience the boys and I had. We stuck together and stayed in control, protecting our land and ourselves from predators—whether we were afraid or not.

ON THE HUNT

We all know the feeling of fear that shoots adrenaline through our veins. It happens when we're faced with the thing that terrifies us most. We must make a split-second decision: fight or flight.

I first met Tanner Webb in 2013 through a mutual friend and an organization that took kids with disabilities out hunting. From the

Tanner Webb, who was born with cerebral palsy, bagged a 175-pound bear with a crossbow on a hunting trip in Canada. Pictured are (from left) David Holder; Tanner; and Tanner's friend Steve Greet.

moment I met Tanner, I knew there was something special about this teenager. He had been born with cerebral palsy and was unable to walk, but he was still determined to hunt. To make matters more complicated, however, his motor skills made it difficult for him to hold his hands steady while trying to shoot his crossbow.

This was a hunt I was destined to remember. Every detail is permanently etched into my mind. The organization that hooked me up with Tanner asked if I would be willing to film his first-ever deer hunt. I was happy to say yes. For two days we tried to position Tanner close enough to get a shot at his first deer. We had no luck. The following year, our family took it upon ourselves to help Tanner get his first deer, and we finally brought his eight-year quest to a successful conclusion.

After the hunt was over, I decided to offer him another hunt. I asked him, "If you could hunt anything, what would it be?"

"A bear," he replied, "but I'm kind of scared of them."

Now the wheels in my head were turning. Maybe it was part of my destiny to help Tanner overcome his fear of bears.

I invited Tanner and his dad to Buck Country Outfitters in Canada to hunt the animal he feared most. I wasn't sure which was greater, his fear of bears or my fear of failing him. All I knew was that we were both about to be tested. When we arrived in Canada, Tanner's dad wheeled him into the hunting lodge.

As they crossed the threshold, Tanner spotted the beautiful blond bearskin rug stretched across the floor, and his face clouded with apprehension. To the kid's credit, he didn't let the sight of those teeth and claws scare him off. He recovered quickly, and as with most boys of his age, there was a glimmer of excitement shining through the fear in his eyes.

Just as a soldier never goes into battle without preparing mentally, a hunter doesn't hit the trail without being fully prepared either. Tanner trusted me to haul him deep into the Canadian bush and set him, in a wheelchair, 20 yards from food strategically placed to draw in the animal he feared most. To succeed on this bear hunt, he would have to turn his fear into focus. (I would have to do the same.) There was no room for error.

Facing your fear is easy to talk about but hard to do. I wasn't scared of the hunt—I was afraid I wouldn't be able to help make Tanner's dream of killing a bear come true. And of course, his safety was foremost on my mind. Due to his disability, this situation was anything but typical. Success demanded we adjust our approach to this hunt with Tanner's unique challenges in mind. I knew Tanner could make the shot. I just had to get him in position to take it.

The following morning, Tanner's anxiety was evident. Over breakfast, he rattled off questions as fast as he could manage. Would we take shotguns as backup? What if a bear climbed into the blind with us? He talked more than he ate. I finally realized why he was so afraid. I could run from a bear if the situation called for it, but Tanner couldn't even walk. If left to his own devices, what could he do if something went wrong? The fear factor for him was at a different level. Anxiety about facing a bear for someone with full control of every muscle would be bad enough. I could only imagine Tanner's fear. He would be sitting just a few feet away from an animal weighing hundreds of pounds, an animal with the ability to take a human life in a matter of seconds. This kid was braver than he knew.

His dad and I both tried to reassure him. But the fact that either of us would give our life before we'd let Tanner be mauled by a bear wasn't really the issue. Fear is like that. It grips your gut and shoots what-ifs to your brain. There's not a whole lot you can do but face it head-on.

If you don't face your fear, it can cripple you. But harnessing the power of fear can propel you forward into adventures you never dreamed possible. What you are afraid of doesn't matter; what matters is how you handle it. Tanner Webb was determined to harness his fear, and the result would be life changing.

We settled into the blind, hoping today would be the day Tanner took his first bear. We hadn't been there long when I heard a limb crack. My heart pounded in my ears, making it difficult to tell which direction the noise was coming from. I could see flashes of black dipping in and out of the timber in front of us.

Tanner's breathing accelerated, and I could sense his tension. I could imagine his heart must be slamming against his chest the same way mine was. As a 175-pound bear appeared to my left, his excitement grew, and I'm pretty sure fear was the last thing on his mind. The bear cautiously moved down the trail toward the blind. The bear stopped 17 yards away. This was Tanner's big chance. With a deep inhale, he lined up his crossbow…

Zing.

The arrow passed through the vitals of the bear, sending a red spray into the air. A perfect shot! Tanner was all smiles, and so was I. He had done it.

Tanner had killed a bear, but that wasn't all. He had faced his greatest fear, and in the process, he discovered that what he feared most wasn't nearly as terrifying as he thought.

We waited in the blind just to make sure the bear was dead.

I clapped the proud boy on the shoulder the way I would have congratulated Warren or Easton. "You know who I bet is looking down today and cheering you on?" I asked. According to Tanner and his dad, Tanner's mom, Amy, had loved her son more than anything in this world. She'd always been his biggest cheerleader—which explained a lot about how Tanner had the tenacity to face his fear and do what a lot of grown men wouldn't have attempted. Sadly, two years before, Amy had gone to work and, at lunchtime, had laid her head down on her desk and passed from this life into the next. Without warning, and only in her forties, she suffered a massive heart attack.

"She'd be proud." Tanner's eyes shimmered with unshed tears. "She also would have wanted to come with us. Her worrying about me would've ruined all the fun."

We found Tanner's bear less than 50 yards from where he had taken the shot. Its coat was coal black and made a beautiful rug. Tanner's fear of bears, and my fear of failing him, had both been conquered. Thank you, Tanner, for helping me realize that fear turned into focus is a good thing. Thanks for reminding me that life begins where fear ends.

BEYOND THE HUNT

Tanner's dad, Kevin, and a family friend had joined Tanner on this six-day bear hunt. After Tanner killed his bear, they decided to hunt as well. We didn't film those hunts, but they both ended up killing really nice bears. I was now the only one in our group who hadn't been hunting, which was fine—Tanner's success was all that had really mattered to me. On the fourth day, Brandon, the outfitter guiding us, approached me and asked if I wanted to try my luck. I hadn't intended to hunt this time around, but Brandon was convincing. "There's a really big bear we've been trying to kill for four years. You can hunt him if you want," he said. There was no way I could resist that challenge.

Adam, our production manager, decided to go along with me so he could get some additional camera footage of bears coming and going for the episode we were filming. The hunting guide told us where to go and what to look for: "The bear you're after is following a sow. You'll know it's her because she's missing all her hair. Once you spot her, he won't be far behind."

We sat on the ground with brush stacked around us. Within two hours, we'd seen five or six bears, but not the hairless sow or the big boar we were after.

Suddenly, the worst-case scenario happened. It's the only time in my life I've been terrified of an animal. A different sow came through the woods with four little football-sized cubs. Things had just gotten real. You don't need to be told why. There's a good reason for the term "mama bear"; those ladies are constantly watching for the smallest threat. They're ready to defend their little ones with a ferocity that is unparalleled in the animal kingdom.

I barely breathed as she fed around a little bit and then left. You can imagine the sense of relief that washed over me as I watched her four cubs follow her away from our location. But my relief was short-lived. Right before dark, we saw her again. She made her way back to our makeshift ground blind, but this time on a course that would take her right past us. At less than eight yards, she stopped, face to face with us, trying to figure out what we were. I was rattled but tried to sit still. I thought she would lose interest and move along. But almost before we could blink, everything changed. One of the cubs moved away from her and headed straight toward us. Our guide had forgotten to leave us a shotgun—if she charged, we were pretty much at her mercy.

The cub was now at my feet. If he kept coming...Well, let's just say I could practically feel the sow's claws tearing into me.

The cub sniffed, inching closer to me. I didn't move a muscle. If I had, you probably wouldn't be reading this right now. In an instant that I can attribute only to the intervention of God, the mama bear gave a "woof," calling her cub. Immediately, he spun his chubby little body around and loped back to her feet.

My brain barely had time to register relief as she led the four cubs back the way they'd come. We sat for a while, trying to wrap our heads around the fact that we weren't in the grip of one of nature's most powerful creatures. Thankfully, God is even more powerful than a mama bear with a curious baby.

The next day, I was supposed to go back to the same spot. This time Adam couldn't come with me, so I would be sitting by myself. After the events of the previous day, I was apprehensive. Still, I agreed to go, but I made it very clear to the outfitter that I expected him to leave me a shotgun. After getting set up in the same spot, I looked around. No shotgun. Frustrating as it was, there was nothing I could do but keep an arrow handy and hope I had enough time to defend myself.

Over the next few hours, I saw about 20 different bears, including a 300-pounder that came within 12 yards. But so far, I hadn't caught even a glimpse of the hairless sow or the mammoth bear rumored to be following her like a lovesick puppy.

With bears crashing through the brush and climbing trees all around me, I wished like crazy the outfitter hadn't left me out there without a gun—for the second day in a row. Having a handy arrow gave me a measure of peace, but not enough. I saw a ton of bears.

Close to the end of the day, I suddenly caught movement from the corner of my eye. There she was—that beautiful, bald girl walking in my direction. I remembered the outfitter telling me if I saw her to be ready because the bear I was after would be hot on her trail. So I nocked an arrow. Sure enough, he wasn't far behind. He was huge, at least two feet taller than any other bear I had seen. He came near and stopped.

Instead of shooting right away, I reached for the camera. No way did I want to miss the chance to film this guy. Fumbling around and trying to get a good camera angle, I missed my shot.

Disappointed, I watched him move away. There were less than ten minutes of light left in the day. I figured the hunt was over. Then I perked up, my pulse rising as I saw what I thought was the same bear coming back. He kept advancing until he entered bow range. I came to full draw. But just before I found my shot, he dropped to the ground. I let down my bow as he lay there facing me. Suddenly, without warning, he lumbered to his feet and ran off.

Before I could wrap my head around his strange behavior, I heard something to my right. Standing approximately 20 yards from me was the first bear I had been after. I realized I had almost shot the wrong bear. The original bear—the biggest bear I had ever seen—was cautiously approaching again. I slowly raised and drew my bow, heart hammering against my chest. The arrow found its mark. Down he went.

The bear weighed 412 pounds and, at the time, was the largest ever killed in that location. I hadn't gone on this hunt to kill a bear, but I ended up taking a giant. It was a once-in-a-lifetime blessing that I would never have been given had I not been determined to help Tanner overcome his fear and achieve his dream of killing a bear. I believe God put me in the right place at the right time and caused my arrow to fly straight.

Fear can be paralyzing. If I had allowed fear to take over my mind, I would never have gone back into the woods by myself a second time. The result would have been failure. Fear will keep you from truly living.

So how do you turn fear into focus? I'm an old-school thinker, so my answer is going to be simple: You'll find freedom from fear when you begin to see yourself doing whatever it is that terrifies you. If fear begins in your mind, replace that fear with absolute focus and determination to face it. What if you started blocking your fear by keeping the result you hope to achieve front and center? That's a game-changer!

KARIN | I once had a massive fear of getting into tree stands because of their height. You can imagine how problematic that could be for a professional hunter.

One instance comes to mind. As the boys got a bit older, I started to go hunting with David more often. At the time, we still lived in Montana and were going whitetail deer hunting in the town of Choteau. We were not yet filming our hunts, so David and I sat in separate trees. In Montana, the wind blows all the time. On this day, the wind was absolutely howling, bending the tops of the trees.

We walked up to the tree where he was going to drop me off. I took a deep breath, knowing it was time to do what I had been dreading all day. I was too stubborn to admit how terrified I was, but I hesitated, staring up at the swaying stand. David's eyebrows rose while he looked at me as if to say, "Any day now."

I knew I had to do it or chicken out. Somehow, I mustered the courage to begin the climb. This stand didn't have a ladder but rather tree-stand steps, so I had to hug the tree as I went up. I finally made it into the stand. Looking down at him, I said, "Okay, I'm good. See you later." Mind you, I had not gotten my bow ready, hung up my pack, or anything else. We used safety belts at the time, not harnesses. That meant if I fell out of the tree, I needed enough upper-body strength to turn myself right-side up.

David was hesitant about leaving me. He asked one more time, "Are you sure you're okay?"

"I'm good." I'm pretty sure he heard me gulp as the tree swayed from side to side.

"You know, you're going to have to let go of that tree if you're going to shoot a deer."

My heart was beating out of control, but I still smiled, pretending there wasn't a major problem happening in the tree stand. David can always tell when I'm offering less than the full truth. He wasn't about to leave me. He stayed planted until I gave up my stubbornness and climbed back down.

I learned that day that if I wanted to be a successful hunter, I had to get over my fear of heights and tree stands. I took action. I started hunting from tree stands more often. I used a ladder stand instead of climbing sticks or tree-stand steps to help me feel more secure during the climb. These small adjustments went a long way in helping me get comfortable with being off the ground. Eventually I began to move around while in the stand, trusting that it was properly secured and that I was safe.

Now I don't even think about it. In fact, I like being in a tree better than being on the ground or in a blind. I can see better, and the animals don't know I'm there. It's peaceful and serene. I love it!

DAVID | My faith hasn't always played a starring role in conquering my fears. When I was younger, I tried to handle life by myself. I believed I could do anything I set my mind to if I worked hard enough. Sometimes I was lucky enough to make it past the obstacle I was facing, but it was a gamble at best. Now I realize the role Jesus plays in helping me with my fear. For example, I did a lot of praying the day I had the encounter with the sow and four cubs. I've learned that when it comes to overcoming my fear or anything else, I can't do it on my own. The good news is that I don't have to.

It takes away a lot of pressure when you realize that there is someone bigger and greater than you in this world and that the outcome doesn't have to be determined by your ability to handle the situation. Even when I don't understand what's happening in my life, I still believe God has a plan, and because of that plan, I don't have to be afraid of the future.

Look at it like this: If you're lost in the woods alone, the level of fear you experience will be through the roof. But if you're lost in the woods with someone else, the fear factor will be far less. Just having someone there to talk to and help you figure out the way to go makes all the difference. Jesus will be to you in life what your hunting buddy would be to you if you were lost in the woods. You can ask Him what He thinks and how to safely move forward. Jesus will remind you of what fear is trying to convince you to forget. That He is with you. He'll never leave or forsake you.

If you believe someone is always there to help you, you'll never feel alone. When facing fear, the temptation is to forget about your faith and allow panic to take over. I've been there. Sometimes I still find myself struggling to trust God when I'm afraid and don't know what to do. I'm learning to pray about it instead of worry. My prayer is that you will do the same.

KARIN | Like David, I believe faith helps us overcome fear. For me, conquering fear begins when I admit to God that I'm human and need His help. I've learned to trust Him and believe He's got my back. Keep in mind that God is kind, loving, and patient. The more you talk to Him about your shortcomings, the more He'll support and lead you in the right direction. I had no real reason to be afraid of heights or tree stands; I was just unfamiliar and unskilled.

Fear holds you back and keeps you from doing what God intends for you to do. If I hadn't allowed God to help me with my fear of tree stands, I'm not sure what role I'd be playing at *Raised Hunting*. I know I wouldn't be in front of the camera as often. My fear would have set limits around me.

Facing your fear is never easy, but neither is anything worth doing.

Don't give up, and if you fall out of the tree, climb back up. Staying at the bottom will get you nowhere.

> *Don't panic. I'm with you. There's no need to fear*
> *for I'm your God. I'll give you strength. I'll help*
> *you. I'll hold you steady, keep a firm grip on you.*
> **ISAIAH 41:10 MSG**

ANCHOR POINTS

- If you don't face your fear, it can cripple you. Harnessing the power of fear can propel you forward into adventures you never dreamed possible.
- Pray about it; don't worry about it.
- You can conquer fear when you begin to see yourself doing what terrifies you.
- Conquering fear begins where self-reliance ends.
- Fear holds you back and keeps you from fulfilling God's purpose.

CONFESSION FIRE

Fear can stop you dead in your tracks when you refuse to confront what terrifies you. Consider what you fear most. Why? What steps will you take to overcome it?

KARIN'S GAME PLAN

ANTELOPE TENDERLOIN APPETIZER

This crostini appetizer is great for the holidays!

INGREDIENTS

8 oz. antelope tenderloin
4 cloves garlic
teriyaki sauce
fresh black ground pepper
pink Himalayan salt
1 or 2 loaves Italian bread (small diameter)
basil olive oil
Parkay spray
1 tomato
1 to 1½ T. reduced-fat garlic and herb soft spreadable cheese
chives

DIRECTIONS

1. Wild-game tenderloin is best if it's eaten fresh and has never been frozen. Clean the tenderloin, trim away any tissue, and place the meat in a gallon-size freezer bag.

2. Add 1 diced garlic clove, teriyaki sauce, pepper, and salt until the meat is covered (use your own judgment).

3. Marinate the tenderloin for 24 to 48 hours.

4. Warm a barbecue grill to medium heat and cook the tenderloin on each side 4 minutes before removing. (Meat will be medium rare.)

5. Slice the tenderloin into thin strips and set aside.

6. Warm the oven to 425 degrees.

7. Slice the Italian bread into thin slices.

8. Brush basil olive oil lightly across the top of the bread and then place oil-side down on a cookie sheet.

9. Spray the top side of the bread with Parkay spray.

10. Bake in the oven for 5 to 8 minutes or until the bread is crisp.

11. Pull the bread out of the oven and let cool for a couple minutes.

12. Rub a garlic clove over the top of the bread.

13. Spread the soft garlic cheese over the bread.

14. Rub a tomato slice over the bread or lay a slice on the bread (either way works).

15. Lay a thin slice of tenderloin on top of the tomato and sprinkle chives on top.

NUTRITION

Serving size—2 crostini
Calories—74
Fat—2.5 grams
Carbohydrates—3.9 grams
Protein—8.4 grams

6

DECISIONS

Living with Your Choices

KARIN | As we lay in the tent, I could hear thunder echoing off the distant mountainside. I thought it would pass. After all, it had been a beautiful, early September day in Montana. And before we had left the house, I had checked the weather. There was no indication of storms in the forecast. Not even drizzle.

David, two-year-old Warren, and I had spent the day hiking and looking for signs of moose. Most hunters apply for a tag and then wait for several years before actually being drawn for one, but I had been lucky enough to get a tag after living in Montana just two years. I was beyond excited at this opportunity.

The thunder continued. The closer it got, the more nervous I became. We had only our little tent to keep the rain off, and we had no experience with mountain thunderstorms. If you've ever been out west, you're probably already aware of how Mother Nature makes sure you know who is in charge. She can change things on a whim.

It was about 8:00 p.m. when the heavy rain arrived. Lightning streaked across the sky like an Olympic sprinter, and the thunder shook the mountain underneath us. The rain came in waves. One minute it was terrifying, and the next we felt relieved, believing we would stay safe.

I began to wonder if we could be struck by lightning in the tent.

Surprisingly, Warren was calm, but I was getting more and more uncomfortable. The storm continued for the next three hours. It was relentless. Later, I was told that storms in the mountains of Montana usually roll in fast and leave the same way, but this one was not letting up. At 11:00 p.m. the tent started to leak, and it was getting cold. David and I decided we needed to get in the truck as soon as possible to stay dry and wait for the storm to pass. The situation had become unsafe for all of us. Once we were in the truck, however, the storm intensified and things went from bad to worse. I was no longer just uncomfortable— I was flat-out scared.

Karin Holder, in her early hunting days.

At 1:00 a.m., we decided to try to drive our way down the mountain through the storm. There was a small town about 20 miles away, and we would have to drive through the canyon to get there.

As we approached the tiny town, the storm was suddenly gone. It was as if God said, "Okay, that's enough now." In Montana, the smallest towns are just like you see in Western movies, with tumbleweeds rolling down the road, the wind whistling, and storefronts all facing one another. This town was so small it had one gas station, one bar, and one auto-body shop. That was it. By now, it was 2:00 a.m., and we were certain we would have no luck finding a room.

As we pulled into the bar parking lot, we noticed a light inside. We knocked, and a woman came to the door. I explained our situation and asked if she had a place where we could stay until daylight. She had one room in the back of the bar we could rent. We gladly accepted her offer.

Here's the odd part: As we drove into town, we noticed there was no sign of rain, thunder, or lightning. It felt like we had imagined the entire storm. While we puzzled over the absence of even a mud puddle, we noticed a car pulling into the bar parking lot. A young girl got out and asked us if we knew where a gas station was. She was a college student traveling home for the weekend and was dangerously close to running out of gas. She was not going to make it to the next station. In addition, the next day was Sunday, and the station in this town would not be open. We invited her to stay the rest of the night with our family so she would be safe and off the highway.

The next day, we woke up to find the young lady gone and a thank-you note on the chair. At first light, she had found someone at the bar with enough gas to get her to the next town. David, Warren, and I made our way back to our camping spot and continued our search for moose. (I didn't kill one on that hunt, but I got one later that season. David will give you all the fun details in chapter 9.)

The entire incident with the storm seemed odd and out of place. I couldn't figure it out. Finally, I realized that God knew this young girl was in trouble. He also knew no one would be around on those lonely mountain roads at that time of the morning (at least no one who was up to anything good). I believe He created the storm and increased the intensity and pressure until we finally got the message. The thunder and lightning weren't meant to scare us, but to get us out of the mountains just in time to meet up with this young lady and provide a safe place for her to stay.

I still get chills when I reflect on that night. It makes me listen not only to what God is saying but also to what He is doing. Our decision to come off that mountain wasn't based on blue sky, but on a storm sent by God.

ON THE HUNT

DAVID | As Warren and Easton pulled into the garage, Karin and I knew something was up. We were preparing for our next hunt just as the boys were returning from one. Once out of the ATV, I heard Warren say, "You won't get another chance like that; I guarantee it."

"With my luck, maybe I will," Easton insisted.

Warren was visibly upset and Easton a little shaken. Clearly our sons were arguing about something that had gone down during their hunt. Like most parents, Karin and I allow our boys to work out their own conflicts, but this situation seemed like more than a simple argument. I wanted to know what happened.

Easton began the explanation, stating his side of the issue: "We saw a really big deer. He was close too—less than 20 yards. When I drew my bow, something went wrong, and I couldn't see my pins. So I didn't take the shot."

Warren wasn't buying it. He insisted that the 150-inch buck was close enough to shoot regardless. As I listened to the two of them bickering back and forth, I realized Easton had made the only decision he could live with, even if his brother disapproved.

Decisions are easy to avoid but impossible to ignore. Like dominoes, each choice has the potential to affect the next. If you're like me, sometimes you wrestle with whether you're making the right ones.

David Holder with the elusive deer known as the Big Eight.

Any way you choose, actions have consequences that can take years to work your way through—good or bad. Even doing nothing is a decision. The important thing is realizing you will have to live with your choice.

Life, like hunting, is about more than simply making an important decision; it's about living with your decisions. Easton's new glasses had fogged, and his peep sight had slightly twisted, causing him to feel uncomfortable about the shot. He was right not to take it. Warren, not realizing what had happened, couldn't seem to keep from digging at him about not shooting.

Anyone who knows my family also knows we take hunting and the killing of animals very seriously. We treat every animal and every shot with dignity and respect. We spend countless hours on the archery range, trying to perfect our skills. I've taught my boys that when it comes to hunting, we must live by one rule: If you aren't sure you can make the shot, don't take it. (And in this case, don't pay any attention to what your brother has to say.)

During this season, I too would learn a valuable lesson. A deer we had previously known only through our trail cameras finally made his way into one of our food plots—the deer we called the Big Eight. Realizing I had a chance to hunt the elusive buck would change all my decisions for the rest of bow season. The quest for the Big Eight had begun.

But here's the lesson: When you make the decision to go after that one prize, you also commit to not shooting any other deer. I had passed on a lot of really nice bucks that Karin and the boys would have shot. For me, it was the Big Eight or nothing. He wasn't the largest on our farm, but there was something about the configuration of his rack that I couldn't get out of my mind. You've probably had a similar experience with a deer that isn't the biggest in the woods but is just unique enough to be unforgettable. The Big Eight was that and more.

As the days passed, I finally had the right wind to hunt in a turnip patch on a piece of ground we call the Eighty. I was alone in a ground blind, which meant that if the opportunity presented itself, I would also have to run the camera. I hadn't been there long before I saw a tall, heavy set of antlers on the edge of the food plot. It was him! I picked up a set of rattling horns and began crashing them together. The Big Eight jerked his head up and spun around to see where the noise was coming from. I continued to rattle the horns, louder this time. Now convinced there were other bucks in the area, he began to trot in my direction. He came on a string and dipped into some brush before disappearing. He had outsmarted me again, but I knew where he was, and that's where I determined I'd be every day until the end of the season.

After several more failed attempts, I was back in the turnip plot on the last day of the season. So was he. If I didn't get him now, I wouldn't have another chance until the following year.

As he grazed on turnips, I could see the clump of grass I had marked earlier with my range finder. It was at 40 yards. If he made it to that spot, I'd shoot. Just before I drew back my bow, he turned and walked away. My heart dropped.

He had done exactly what he was supposed to do—what I had planned for—by passing through the sorghum into the open field. In my perfect scenario, he'd have walked straight within range. But he didn't. He stopped two yards short of where I felt comfortable shooting. Looking back, I just couldn't convince myself that it was worth taking the risk of injuring him. It didn't feel right, and even though this was the deer of my dreams, I felt good about my decision to let him walk away.

Weeks earlier, Warren had taunted Easton for not taking a shot at a deer. I remember listening as my younger son defended his decision, but admittedly, I had never really put myself in his shoes. Now I could tell him about the shot I didn't take. The Big Eight, the buck of my dreams, had just walked in and out of my life, and I hadn't been able to release a single arrow.

I understood how Easton must have felt, and I realized it was never about making the decision; it was about living with it. Little did I know this would not be my last encounter with the Big Eight…

BEYOND THE HUNT

I've made some hard choices while out hunting, but in the grand scheme of things, those choices were insignificant. The choices I make in life, the ones that affect my family and me, are of far greater importance.

Most people don't know the David Holder who drank like a fish. I grew up just outside of Washington, DC, in a family that struggled mightily with alcoholism. My uncles, brother, and grandfather were all successful businessmen, making a fortune in construction. They were also alcoholics who drank away every dime. Too many times to count, I watched those guys—my male role models—walk into a bar and buy a round for the entire house because they had just cashed a large check.

I look back today and realize how different things could have been for them. They would have likely been multimillionaires if they had not allowed alcohol to take over their lives. Instead, one of them rolled a truck, killing two friends. Another drove into a telephone poll, ending his life. One got liver cancer. My brother shot himself at 29 years old, and my grandfather was killed in an alcohol-related incident as well.

As a young man, I was following in their footsteps. Even though I loved hunting, I was often too hungover to even get up and go on a hunt. At the time, my uncles were paying me good money to work for them, so buying alcohol wasn't a problem. My friends and I worked during the day and drank at night. That was our life. I was young and having a good time—or so I thought.

I can't remember exactly when it happened—I think it was around the time my brother committed suicide—but I eventually realized I was going down the same path as the other men in my family, a life of working hard and drinking even harder. I had idolized my brother and looked up to him more than anyone else. But I knew I didn't want to come to the same end. I needed to start making better decisions, and for the first time in my life, I was ready to do just that.

I realized I needed to get away from the familiar, to make a fresh start. I had a job opportunity in Arkansas, and I believed that moving there would provide the change in environment I needed.

Karin and I were engaged to be married, but we were battling because she was hesitant about coming with me. Finally, I told her I had to go because if I stayed I would end up just like my family. I'm thankful Karin agreed to come as well. My parents drove to Arkansas to help us move. Like a couple of giddy kids, Karin and I sneaked off to the justice of the peace and got married. We thought my parents would be overjoyed. Instead, my mom was terribly upset. It was a full year before she spoke another word to me. Later in life, I would understand her reasoning and why our actions had hurt her. The year before, she had lost her oldest son, and now her youngest had not included her in his wedding. At the time, in my eyes, her actions just didn't make sense. But after raising my own kids, I can see more clearly what caused her pain.

After my parents left, Karin and I were on our own for the first time. I was still struggling with alcohol but was now ready to confront my addiction. I wish I could have stopped drinking cold-turkey. But for me, it was more of a gradual climb out. Even though I didn't go to church, I knew enough about God to pray and ask for help. Without His help, I seriously doubt I'd have ever had the strength to become sober. Now I can look back and say that the decision to move to Arkansas in 1992 saved my life. On December 7, 1998, I took my last drink.

KARIN | Easton was comfortable choosing not to shoot that deer, but not all decisions leave us feeling that way. To me, the most important thing regarding a decision is that you make one. Whether it's right or wrong, you must act, or nothing ever happens.

As I write this, I'm smack-dab in the middle of one of the most important decisions of my life. If it is the right decision, good things will happen: Our company will grow, and we will continue to provide opportunities to our many employees. Our impact on the lives of the viewers and fans of *Raised Hunting* will become greater, and the number of those who can learn the life lessons we teach through time spent in the outdoors will multiply. I feel confident we've listened correctly to the messages God is sending us. Our boys will have the opportunity to continue growing in the hunting industry, and to develop and gain unparalleled experience from living this life.

On the other hand, as I look at David today, I can see he's scared out of his mind. His body language is telling me he's questioning whether we're doing the right thing by leaving our network of almost five years to take the leap to the Discovery Channel—the largest network that airs outdoor programming. I've been an advocate for this move. I've looked at all the pros, cons, and business opportunities, and I think it's our best option. If it fails, I'll have to own it. Bottom line: This could be the best thing that has ever happened to us, or it could be a disaster that could ruin everything we've worked so hard to build together.

So I'm staying positive and focusing on the "why." Why are we doing this? My prayer has been, "God, if this is Your will, then tell us, because we're in it together." I realize that even when something is God's will, it won't be without challenges. There will be bumps along the way. I also understand that when it comes down to it, the only things we really have in this life are our relationship with God and family and our love for others.

The crazy thing about all this is that we don't have to take the risk— I could easily continue to work in my financial career, as I have for the past 14 years. It provides a stable income. That would be the safe, comfortable thing to do, not to mention that I love helping people achieve their financial goals and retirement dreams. However, the decision to switch networks impacts an even greater number of people, as we will have a larger reach. This decision gives kids like Jack Quinlan hope.

Jack is 17 years old and has cancer. He reached out to let us know that our show about a family hunting together gave him hope. Even though Jack is battling for his life, he still wants to meet David and Karin Holder of *Raised Hunting*. This makes me feel both humbled and heartbroken at the same time. There are many more kids like Jack out there, and by enlarging our audience, we just might be able to reach them.

I'm digging down. I'm lifting my husband up and encouraging him even though I am terrified. I'm letting him know that I support him as I always have. And he is doing the same for me. The darkness sitting on my shoulder, telling me that we're going to fail, is only there to get in the way of us impacting people like Jack. I'm not willing to listen to that negative voice.

Decisions are hard, but we are forced to make them anyway. We must trust the Lord by acting—we call it a "step of faith"—or nothing will change.

If you're stuck, keep moving, even when you want to give up.

DAVID | I can be stubborn. Sometimes I learn the hard way, but I'm finally realizing how much easier life is when I allow God to help with my decisions. I'll admit that, in the past, I've tried to work around God instead of working with Him, and I believed I could do most of what needed to be done with the two hands He gave me. I've recently learned, however, that the decisions God helps me with always turn out better than the ones I make on my own.

With the filming of *Raised Hunting*, getting to church on Sundays can be difficult. I just figured God understood. After all, He knew we had a signed contract and had to film these hunting shows. But Karin wasn't having it. We constantly fought over whether we were going to church on Sunday or if we were going to work on *Raised Hunting*. For years it was a source of contention between us.

One day, I was discussing this with a friend, complaining about how unreasonable she was. He said something to me I will never forget. "After all God has done for you and blessed you with, and you can't even give up a couple of hours on Sunday to thank Him?" I had never really looked at it that way, but his words made sense.

Karin always insisted that if I went to church with her and the boys, God would help me get more done in less time. I had a hard time getting that idea through my head. God had given me two hands and a job to do. Besides, what better place to talk with God than out in nature? Both thoughts were valid, but I realized they were misguided.

When our entire family goes to church on Sunday, we get along better, and as Karin said, we accomplish more in a shorter amount of time. My decisions are clearer, and there's less pressure when I feel connected to a spiritual family. I don't have it all figured out yet, but I'm working on it. I love waking up on Sunday morning and feeling like I belong somewhere other than in the woods hunting. You can always hunt after church!

Commit your actions to the LORD, and your plans will succeed.
PROVERBS 16:3 NLT

ANCHOR POINTS

- God can speak to you without using words.
- Like hunting, life is about more than making decisions. It's about living with your decisions.
- Being in God's will doesn't mean there won't be challenges along the way.
- Decisions are hard. Make them anyway.

CONFESSION FIRE

Life is full of scary decisions. Consider the decisions in front of you. What are they? What will you do to move forward?

KARIN'S GAME PLAN

PERMISSION BROWNIES

David and I have hunted together for more than 25 years. We have gained permission to hunt on *a lot* of property. Looking the landowner in the eye, being respectful, and having a conversation might have gotten us permission to hunt all those places, but my brownies helped us keep it! We take these to all our landowners to thank them for allowing us to hunt. This little gesture goes a long way and has never failed us. Try it; it works.

Warning—this is not a low-fat, healthy recipe!

INGREDIENTS

1 box Betty Crocker Supreme
    Triple Chunk Brownie Mix
1 box Betty Crocker Fudge
    Brownie Mix
½ bag Ghirardelli milk chocolate
    chips

2 whole eggs
2 egg whites
½ cup water (do not use oil)

DIRECTIONS

1. Preheat the oven to 350 degrees.
2. Mix all the ingredients in a large bowl with a wooden spoon.
3. Spray a 9 × 13-inch pan with Pam.
4. Spoon the brownies mix into the pan.
5. Bake for 28 minutes.

Bake the brownies for a shorter amount of time than the box calls for so they are fudgy. You will need to test this with your own oven. Cook to desired doneness.

Taking the oil out of the mix doesn't do anything except make the brownies better, and it leaves out the oil taste. No need for applesauce or any other replacement.

NUTRITION

Calories—268
Fat—5.5 grams
Carbohydrates—56 grams
Sugars—36 grams
Protein—2 grams

7

THE BIG EIGHT

Waiting

DAVID | I was 16 years old when I picked up a bow and arrow for the first time. I was hooked instantly and still am. There was something about holding that bow in my hand that I can't explain. Even though the bow was old and not very accurate, I fell in love with the idea of bowhunting. It wasn't until I was 18 that I found a bow that hit where I was aiming. I remember standing in my basement the day it arrived from Bass Pro. I tried to pull it back but couldn't. I didn't realize it was cranked all the way up to its 60-pound maximum. In a panic, I called a friend whose dad bowhunted. I asked if he could help me. Once he adjusted the draw length and draw weight, allowing me to get to full draw, I began to practice shooting.

When bow season arrived, I had nowhere to hunt. It was a two-hour drive to the national forest, and I didn't know anyone who would allow me to hunt on their private land. Frustrated, I began to look for other options. That's when I found a local hunting club. It was $225 to join— practically a fortune for a kid my age. I sat down with my dad and discussed whether I should spend that much money. Finally, I decided joining the hunting club was my only option if I wanted to bowhunt that year. They had a piece of property I could hunt on just outside of town. It included a gun range but also had 100 acres of woods no one else wanted to hunt.

Until now, I had always bowhunted with my brother. This was the first time I was completely on my own while hunting. I walked a half mile down a railroad right-of-way and then another mile and a half along a power line to where a creek cut across. I looked for deer tracks, and then for some clue as to why the deer would cross there. When I found a small puddle of water in the dry creek bed and fresh white oak acorns littering the ground, I knew I had found the right location. Hanging my deer stand in a straight tree only 12 yards away, I waited. With a perfect wind, it didn't take long for a doe to show up. When she bent down to get a drink from the creek, I let the arrow fly. Shaking and excited, I climbed out of the tree to look for blood but only found a tiny speck. Perplexed, I started following her tracks. I was pretty sure I'd made a good shot, but the small amount of blood concerned me. Had I been too sure of myself? My gut twisted as I followed the trail. Was she wounded and wandering?

I came to a fence, and relief filled me as my uncertainty vanished. She lay just on the other side. I had gotten her. It was a two-mile drag back to the truck, but it was worth every step! I think I scraped all the hair off that deer before getting her loaded, but doing it all by myself made the experience more memorable and more rewarding.

I tell you this because that's where bowhunting began for me. My journey started more than 30 years ago, hunting on property no one else wanted to hunt.

Having now taken more than 200 animals with my bow, I still get just as excited about each hunt as I was the day I killed that doe. We all start somewhere in hunting and in life. The most important thing is not *where* you start but *that* you start.

ON THE HUNT

Life is a series of waiting rooms. You patiently (or not so patiently) wait to get out of one, only to enter the next. You wait for someone to spend your life with, a dream job to come along, your kids to be born, the next big opportunity, or a buck you can't get out of your head.

I think dreams are great, and God often uses them to whet our appetites for the plan He has for us. But what if instead of waiting for the next thing, you started to enjoy where you are right now? I'm slowly learning this, and when it came to the Big Eight, waiting an entire year to hunt him again was one of the hardest things I've ever had to do.

David Holder discusses his successful Big Eight hunt with son Warren.

In my previous encounter with this giant buck, I learned I needed to change my approach. As Easton and I moved the ground blind, I was already planning the next year's strategy out loud. During bow season, I would move the blind closer to where I'd seen the Big Eight enter the radish plot. I also needed to adjust the blend of seeds we were planting. The sorghum had attracted the deer, but the stalks were so tall, I couldn't shoot through them all the way across the field. Easton wasn't convinced the Big Eight would still be around the next year, but something told me I'd get one more chance. At least, that was what I was praying for. All I could do now was wait.

Bowhunting is not just something I do; it's who I am. It's not my hobby; it's my passion. When Karin and I first got married, we occasionally fought about how much I loved hunting. She couldn't understand why I needed to go so much, and I had a hard time explaining it to her. I'm not advocating that you hunt at the expense of your marriage. I'm just being honest about how challenging that part of our marriage was. Sometimes it's difficult to find a balance. Now she loves hunting as much as I do, and with Warren and Easton on board, we have something we can all do together as a family. We really are *Raised Hunting*. It comes as no surprise to me that sometimes I form an emotional bond with the animals I pursue. This was the case with the Big Eight. He was more than just another deer...much more.

I ask myself how a hunter can be so intimately attached to a wild animal, especially after seeing it on only a few rare occasions or catching a picture of it from time to time. Maybe that was my infatuation—the fact that there was no rhyme or reason. The Big Eight had no calendar, clock, or boundaries. He had everything working in his favor, and all I had was the memory of our previous encounter. After bow season, I looked everywhere for a clue of his existence. I hoped and prayed he was still alive but found nothing—not even a shed antler.

The seasons had changed from winter to spring. I finally told myself that with no sign of the Big Eight, it was time to move on. Perhaps the neighbors had gotten him during muzzleloader season. Or, being such a mature buck, he might not have made it through another harsh Iowa winter.

By now, our food plots had been replanted, and I needed to set out the trail cameras so we could put together a list of potential shooter bucks for the fall season. I couldn't find a single camera. Warren was sitting at the dining room table, looking at his computer. I figured he might know where they all went, so I asked him what had happened to them. He gave me a nonchalant glance. "I put them out already."

"Why would you do that?" I asked, frustrated that he hadn't at least let me know first. "You knew I needed some of those for other places."

"Because I knew the Big Eight was still alive!" The excitement in his tone caught my attention.

"What do you mean?"

He pointed to the screen in front of him. "I'm looking at him."

I walked to the table. Sure enough, there he was, only bigger and with more tines. The past year had been very good to the Big Eight, and Warren's trail camera had captured his image. This proved that just when you think you've lost all hope, God can intervene. God had given me another chance at this deer, but I had to make sure to get everything right. The Big Eight was old and smart. It was no accident that he had endured several deer seasons. I would have one shot at this worthy opponent, and I had to make it count.

I've tried to teach my boys that we shouldn't pursue a desire if we have to slight someone else to accomplish it. So even though we knew the Big Eight was out there, I spent the first part of bow season filming for everyone else. Some people believe in karma; I believe that what you give to others will come back to you. The New Testament puts it this way: "A man reaps what he sows" (Galatians 6:7). If I had made the Big Eight the focus of our deer season, my family wouldn't have had as much opportunity to hunt some of the other big bucks on our property. We are a team, and I needed to do what was best for all of us.

November came, and the winds shifted out of the west, creating the perfect conditions to hunt on the Eighty. If I was going to kill the Big Eight, it was now or never. However, there was a slight problem: Even though Easton would be out of school the next day when I intended to hunt, he had to film with Warren for the show, and Karin couldn't get the day off work. So I was on my own. Brendon, a family friend, agreed to join me and film. I could hardly sleep that night in anticipation of the next day's hunt. I'd been waiting an entire year for another chance.

By now, the rut was in full swing, and the bucks were on the move. The weather had been unusually warm that season, with highs in the sixties. But as Brendon and I settled into the ground blind that afternoon, the temperature had dropped, accelerating deer movement. The wind was blowing straight west, which was exactly what I needed so the Big Eight wouldn't pick up our scent. It wasn't long before small bucks and does began trickling into the food plot.

Brendon caught some movement on the ridge in front of us. "I see a buck moving through the brush. Look in the middle of the field and then straight up the hill."

I followed the direction he pointed and caught my breath. The Big Eight was slowly making his way through the scattered timber.

Picking up my rattling horns, I waited for him to move across the hill. I knew if I started rattling while we were in his line of sight, he would see us and go the other direction. Not wanting to spook him, I barely struck the horns together. The sound would make him think a couple young bucks were sparring. The next few seconds felt like an eternity as the tension inside me began to build. Would he respond to the sound and come my way? My chest tightened, my mind racing. I needed to capture every move the deer made. This could be our moment. I said, "Right here, Brendon. Right here. He just stepped out onto the edge of the field."

The Big Eight was now less than 40 yards away and getting closer. All the scouting, waiting, practicing, and agonizing over my last encounter with him were about to come down to one shot. This would probably be my last chance to take this buck, so that one shot had to count. As I came to full draw, he stopped in the turnip patch. This was the opportunity I had imagined, that I had been dreaming about for years.

That's the thing about a long-held dream. Once you decide what's important, you will work toward the outcome you want, even through crushing disappointment—like the year before when I had been so close. You don't stop trying. You look at what doesn't work and fix it—that is, if the dream is big enough. If it matters. In this moment, every thought left my mind except the shot I was about to take. Hope drove me. This was a dream that mattered.

Time slowed as the arrow passed through the air. I watched the glowing blue nock disappear behind his shoulder. The Big Eight whirled around and went back up the hill a few yards before going down. It was hard to breathe or believe what had just happened.

We waited until dark, making sure he was dead before approaching. By now, Karin and the boys had arrived. The blood trail was wide and easy to follow. We walked up the hill right to where he had tipped over. Sure enough, there he was. The deer of my dreams was even bigger than I had imagined. As I put my hands around his antlers for the first time, a lump swelled in my throat, and I blinked away tears of thankfulness. Thankfulness for a family that wanted this for me even more than I wanted it for myself. Thankfulness to God for giving me the opportunity.

To the Big Eight, words will never be able to express how I feel. I'm honored, sad, humbled, and elated. And more than me, this hunt was about you. You lived a full life and will live on in my home for the rest of mine. This is not because I'm morbid or cruel but rather because I owe you the respect to share you with others. I will relive our time together forever. You were more than a worthy opponent. You were more than a deer. You were my obsession. You and I will always be connected. I will miss you, my friend, but I will never forget you. You will always be the Big Eight.

BEYOND THE HUNT

My journey to kill the Big Eight started long before my first encounter with him. It began when I was 18, hunting on the backside of a gun range. I've learned that humble beginnings have a way of taking you to great endings if you stick with the plan and grow along the way. How you start and how you finish shouldn't look the same.

When I first started deer hunting, I just wanted to shoot something—anything. Gradually, I became less excited to shoot anything that moved and more willing to wait for "the big one." Eventually, even that motive changed, and my hunting journey became about giving back to the hunting culture and working to make sure the lifestyle I love so much continues to advance. How I started and where I am now are not the same. And my hunting adventure is still changing and becoming something it's never been.

I've said many times that hunting is my greatest passion. Can you identify your greatest passion? I'm betting you have one. What is that one thing that draws you in and gets most of your focus? There's a good chance that those around you might not be as excited as you are about your passions, but don't let their lack of enthusiasm keep you from pursuing what you can't stop thinking about. If I had done that, *Raised Hunting* would never have happened.

When my brother first started taking me hunting with him, it was more than just fun for me; it was magical. It was all I thought about and what I wanted to do all the time. My greatest childhood memories are of being called to the office in elementary school because my brother was there to pick me up early. When I turned the corner and saw him in the hall wearing a flannel shirt, I knew that meant we were going hunting. I was completely infatuated with every aspect of the outdoors and nature; just seeing a deer from the car on a family trip stirred something inside me.

Whatever your passion and motivation, the only way to get there is hard work. When I first started turkey hunting, I couldn't afford decoys and had no one to teach me how to use a mouth call. So even though I'm not very artistic, I made my first turkey decoys out of cardboard. I went to a turkey farm to listen to the sounds turkeys make so I could mimic them. It was work, but given my resources, it was also the only way to get better at turkey hunting.

Don't be afraid to step out and take initiative, even if you're by yourself. At the time, no one else was making cardboard decoys or sitting beside me outside a barn full of turkeys, but I did those things anyway. To improve, sometimes you must be willing to walk alone. If the dream is big enough and worthy enough, if you want it enough, the price will always be bigger than your resources. That's where God takes up the slack by giving you His ideas, His hope, and the tenacity you never knew you had. Some big dreams are worth a big price tag to achieve.

My only word of caution is that you don't allow your passion to determine the quality of your life. Passion handled correctly can fuel you and make life better, but passion handled incorrectly can take over and ruin everything. I've been guilty of allowing my passion for hunting to affect my relationship with Karin. I'm sure there was a time when she thought I would choose hunting over her. It wasn't true, but I made her feel that way. I was so consumed with hunting that it seemed nothing else mattered, at least in her mind. Most of what I feel qualified to teach are the lessons I had to learn the hard way. Controlling my desire to hunt and not allowing that desire to become more important than God, my marriage, or time with my boys, especially when they were little, took as much work as learning to hunt in the first place.

My passion isn't so much for hunting anymore as it is for the outdoors in general. Spending time outside with my family and capturing their love for hunting on camera so I can share it with you—that's what I enjoy most. Last year, after a successful turkey hunt, Karin raised her turkey up in the air like someone standing on the Olympic podium. Seeing the smile on her face exemplified everything I live for. I guess the lesson is to not be afraid when your passion shifts into something else. Be who you are right now and then fuel that.

KARIN | David certainly waited a long time to get his chance to hunt the Big Eight. I was so proud of him that day, and I'll never forget the look on his face when he finally put his hands on that deer. Waiting is difficult and often frustrating. Our family is no stranger to waiting—sitting in a deer stand, hoping to get a perfect shot, or sitting around the dining room table, discussing when and how to move forward with a big project. Waiting is part of life, and feeling as if you're stuck in limbo can become exhausting. But don't allow the waiting period of the journey to keep you from accomplishing your goal. Even when things appear to be at a standstill, keep moving forward.

I remember when I submitted my request at work to relocate from northwest Montana to the Midwest in order to continue filming *Raised Hunting*. Although our family was mentally ready for a move, the time wasn't right in God's eyes, so we had to remain patient and focused on our goal. It wasn't easy, but we did it by following two action steps.

First, we discussed the what-if scenarios, creating a plan. We had to know what to do if the door opened and what to do if it didn't. Because there were no guarantees, it was important for us to create options either way. Now we had the peace of knowing that no matter what the decision, there was still a path to get us where we wanted to go.

Second, we didn't stop our lives while waiting for the answer. We kept right on living. I continued to serve my clients to the best of my ability while David continued filming and working on our property. Warren and Easton continued to be involved in school and sports. We never allowed ourselves to stagnate while waiting.

When the door did open, we were prepared to move into action. We determined timelines and what needed to be done by when. Then we decided what we needed to finish before we could move on to where we were going next. Months before the "all clear" was given, the wheels had been set in motion. Waiting is much easier when you're busy positioning yourself for advancement. That's what we did.

DAVID | My faith plays a huge role in how I approach waiting without knowing what's next. But it hasn't always been that way. It's one thing when you're forced to wait an entire year for a buck like the Big Eight; it's an entirely different matter when you're waiting on God for answers. While waiting for the Big Eight, I had things to do. Proactive measures to take. But sometimes waiting on God means just that—waiting with your hands in your pockets and not trying to work things out on your own, no matter how long He takes to pony up the answer. Sometimes He doesn't answer because He's waiting for us to ask the right question.

I haven't always had strong faith and haven't always paid attention to God. For years, I beat my head against the wall without really thinking about whether what I wanted was part of God's plan for me. When something didn't work out, it left me frustrated. I never even considered that maybe the reason it didn't go my way was that Karin was praying for God's plan to unfold, and He had something else in mind.

A lot of peace comes with turning your life over to God—even when He doesn't answer your questions the way you hoped He would. Trusting Him with the outcome allows your soul to relax. I've taken a long time to get to this place. I'm talking to God a lot more these days, and I know He is listening.

I regret that I didn't realize this earlier in my life. I sometimes wonder if Warren and Easton understand how important it is to have a personal relationship with Jesus Christ. I haven't always modeled that for them. Thankfully, their mother stepped up to the plate as a genuine model of faith.

My life is better when I depend on someone more than myself. I do believe in myself, and I know that if I'm doing everything I can, God will do what I can't. Maybe not exactly the way I wanted, but His way for me will be right. Take it from the guy who took years to finally conclude that life works best when I'm not trying to force my way or figure things out. It's better to leave the details with God. I'm not completely there yet, but I'm closer than I've ever been.

KARIN | Waiting can be hard, but I believe that God is ultimately in control. I can trust Him with the future. Obviously, waiting and not knowing what comes next are more difficult in some situations than in others; when a loved one is sick or injured and you're waiting for a diagnosis or waiting for them to get well—that's more stressful than a job interview. But whether I'm waiting for something small or something big, I know who is in control of the outcome. Every aspect of my life is in God's hands. I talk to Him constantly about the situation. I plan, and I pray for help. I trust Him to handle whatever it is. There's really nothing I can do anyway except position myself to advance when the time is right. As humans, we tend to believe we make our own way, but I believe God is better at making a way for me than I could ever make for myself.

I'd be lying if I said darkness doesn't sometimes try to nudge its way into the situation, placing doubt and fear in my mind. I picture my mind like a house with many rooms. The more fear and doubt I allow into the house, the more it takes up space and pushes my faith out. So I picture myself closing the door on darkness, fear, and doubt. I say out loud, "Satan, you're not welcome here." Then I close the door on him— and lock the deadbolt. You can do this too. In fact, why don't you do that right now? Mentally walk through the rooms of your situation, turning the lights on and trusting God with the outcome, whatever it might be.

The dream comes through much effort and the
voice of a fool through many words.
ECCLESIASTES 5:3 NASB

ANCHOR POINTS

- When pursuing a dream, the most important thing isn't *where* you start, but *that* you start.
- Life is a series of waiting rooms. Patience is the key.
- You can enjoy where you are right now. You don't have to wait for the next big thing to be happy.
- At any moment, God can intervene and give you another chance.
- Humble beginnings can lead to great endings—if you stick with them.

CONFESSION FIRE

Life can feel frustrating when you're forced into a waiting room. What are you waiting on, and how will you move forward in the meantime?

KARIN'S GAME PLAN

GARLIC PEPPER VENISON
JALAPEÑO BURGERS

INGREDIENTS

2 lbs. ground venison
1 cup jalapeno peppers
½ cup old-fashioned oats
½ cup Egg Beaters

DIRECTIONS

1. Mix all the ingredients in a large bowl.

2. Divide the burgers into 4 oz. patties.

3. Grill to medium.

NUTRITION

Serving size—1 (4 oz.) patty
Calories—149
Fat—1.8 grams
Carbohydrates—8.4 grams
Protein—22 grams

8

YOU

Getting the Most out of Life

DAVID | Sometimes we overlook the obvious. We often don't see awesome opportunities within our reach because we aren't looking in the right place. At least, that's true in my case. After living in Montana for two or three years, I was convinced there just weren't any spots near me to bowhunt mature whitetail. One day, a friend told me about a place in Choteau, Montana, where I could find a bunch of whitetail deer.

Choteau was only 55 miles from my house, so I decided to go check out the Teton-Spring Creek Bird Preserve, where my friend had seen those deer. Since it was a bird preserve of about 2,000 acres, gun hunting wasn't allowed, but bows were fine. The place was crawling with giant whitetails. On any given hunt, I saw more than 100 deer from my stand. On average, I saw five shooter-sized bucks per sit. Most weren't close enough to shoot, but they were still fun to look at. This preserve was hands-down the best place to hunt deer I've ever seen.

This preserve isn't in the mountains but rests along a four-mile flat in the valley. It's not a place where you would expect to see predatory animals, like wolves or grizzly bears. One morning as I was getting out of my truck to go hunt, an older man appeared. He asked me what I was doing, and I told him I was going deer hunting. He looked at me like I was crazy. "You didn't hear about the grizzly bears?"

I hadn't heard a word about bears, but I didn't want him to think I was blowing him off, so I thanked him for the information. To be honest, though, I *did* blow him off. I thought he didn't know what he was talking about. I hunted that morning without any luck and returned after lunch. I decided to move to another location for my evening hunt, so I cut across a field of tall grass. Suddenly, I heard a couple of voices. I looked around until I spotted a wildlife department truck sitting on a hill a few hundred yards away, beside a bunch of bee hives that were torn apart. I was close enough to hear the conservation agent tell someone from the home office to bring a trap because evidence around the destroyed hives pointed to two bears.

I thought back to the conversion I'd had that morning, the warning I'd totally dismissed. Not sure what to do, I kept going. As I approached a deep ditch in front of me, I heard a low growl. The only weapon I had for defense was my bow, so I nocked an arrow and pretty much waited to die. (One arrow would likely do little more than make a grizzly good and mad.) I heard the growl again, but I couldn't see anything.

My heart jumped into my throat as a whitetail buck sprang from the ditch and took off. I figured the bear must have spooked him. I heard the growl for the third time, but no bear followed the deer. I stood there for what seemed like forever before I got the nerve to take a few steps forward. As I approached the ditch, the growling grew louder. I willed my breathing to even out as I scanned the area, planning for the next few minutes in case I had to run for my life. Just ahead of me, the landscape opened. If I could just get there in one piece, I'd be able to take off running in the opposite direction and maybe get home to my family alive.

With every step forward, the bear grew in my mind's eye until, if he'd stood to full height, I envisioned him towering over the trees. I quickened my last two steps, preparing to bolt down the creek.

Sudden movement to my left caught my attention. I turned my gaze and then stopped short. As my mind adjusted to the reality of the situation, rather than the death-defying images I'd conjured up, I felt like a total idiot. What stood there wasn't the gargantuan grizzly I'd built up in my brain—what I had been hearing the entire time was a beaver gnawing on a stick. There were no bared, knifelike teeth or razor-sharp claws. Just a beaver making a lot of noise—noise I had built up in my mind as the predatory sound of a killer beast.

It's hard to get the most out of life when you live in the altered reality others have planted in your imagination. The old man who told me about the grizzlies was the reason I stood paralyzed in the creek, thinking the worst. The only problem I had that day was the one I'd created for myself. I stood there, staring at that stupid beaver, knowing my wife was going to have a field day when I told her all about it. Guess what? I wasn't wrong.

What if your "bear" is nothing more than a beaver gnawing on a stick?

ON THE HUNT

You've heard me say it before: Hunting and life mean something to all of us, but that something is going to be completely different for you and me. What you get out of this life is up to one person, and that person is not your sibling, pastor, parent, or spouse. What you get out of life and out of hunting is completely up to you.

My family and I were gearing up for another antelope hunt in Wyoming. As we loaded the truck, Warren was giving Easton a hard time about missing football practice. Easton had decided he didn't want to play football his senior year in high school, and Warren thought he was making a mistake he would later regret. Easton reminded Warren—a little forcefully—that it wasn't Warren's decision to make. Although Warren was just looking out for his younger brother, at the end of the day, Easton was right.

My boys approach life and hunting very differently. Warren is more dedicated to the hunt. Easton might have more natural talent and instinct, but he just won't spend the time it takes to be great. Easton's approach to hunting is very nonchalant, and he's successful because he pays attention to the little things. Warren, on the other hand, succeeds because he is dedicated and willing to put in the time. He'll wait out an animal until the very end. If Warren were forced to approach hunting like Easton—or vice versa—I have a feeling neither of them would enjoy it enough to stick with it. They receive from hunting, and life in general, what they put into it. Their approach, and the amount of effort they put into each, reflect who they are. And that's okay.

Warren (left) and Easton Holder approach hunting differently, but both have found ways to be successful.

Easton had never killed an antelope, and this would be his first opportunity. On the drive over, Warren was riding him about holding out for a big one, but Easton was happy to shoot the first one to walk by.

As my sons get older, I find myself noticing that the lessons each must learn are more difficult, which means these lessons are also harder to teach them. However, time spent teaching them is time spent together, and Karin and I wouldn't miss that for anything in the world.

On this hunt, time with our boys meant sitting in the middle of nowhere beside a watering hole in a six-foot ground blind. To top it off, the temperature was 100 degrees. We had already decided Easton and Karin would be the first to hunt, while Warren and I would split up to film each of them. That meant Warren and I would have to wait for our chance.

I usually have a lot of patience while waiting, but I hoped we wouldn't have to wait long in the blind. Easton's eyes were already starting to droop. As I've said, he has a laid-back approach that makes him fun to watch. Maybe that's why I enjoy filming him so much.

Before long, a group of young bucks came to drink. They weren't the biggest antelope, but they were nice and would have been a great first kill for Easton. Still, he decided to hold out for something bigger. He smiled, knowing his decision to pass up these bucks meant Warren would have to wait longer to hunt. In Easton's mind, the only thing better than killing a nice antelope was irritating his older brother. Sibling rivalry is alive and well on any hunt, and my sons are not immune.

The next buck that came to the water wasn't as lucky. Easton made a perfect 24-yard shot. We sat tight, hoping another antelope would make it to the pond before dark. Sure enough, a nice buck topped the hill and made his way toward the blind. Now it was my turn. I made quick work of him. Easton and I had two goats on the ground! It was unbelievable—two tags filled on day one of the hunt!

On the third day, Warren and Karin still hadn't released an arrow. I think God may have been teaching Warren a lesson in patience. And maybe a lesson about the wisdom—or foolishness—of picking on his little brother.

There were only three hours left before it would be time to pack up and head for home. I was filming Karin in the blind while the boys tried a less traditional approach. They had brought a giant cut-out of a black cow, and their plan was to spot some antelope out in the field and walk up to them behind the cut-out, pretending to be a cow! If all went as planned, Warren just might get close enough to shoot.

Imagine two boys, giggling and walking side by side, pretending to be a black cow. That was the scene playing out in front of us. As we watched from a distance, there was an antelope just ahead of them, feeding under a power line. They stopped so Warren could get his bow ready. The buck wasn't spooked, and their plan was working. After a few more steps, they stopped again. This time, Warren was at full draw and released an arrow. Perfect shot. Karin and I watched the boys jumping up and down in celebration as the buck made a death circle before crashing hard on the gravel road beside them. Two boys, one "cow," and a goat made for a great afternoon hunt. Karin also took a nice buck that afternoon. All four of us had tagged out.

Hunting is not just *like* life for us—it *is* our life. It means more to us than we can possibly describe. Each member of the Holder family took away something different from this hunt. For Easton, it was about having to make the right decision—take the first, easiest buck, or be patient and wait for something better to come along. Warren learned the difference between selfishness and selflessness. For Karin it was about meat in the freezer and the time spent with her boys. For me, it was about all that—and the moments the four of us will never forget. Hunting, life lessons, food, and family. What else is there?

BEYOND THE HUNT

We certainly got more out of that antelope hunt than we bargained for. I can't remember another time (other than while turkey hunting) when all four of us got to pose in a single picture with our animals. On that three-day hunt, life gave us more than we expected. I think there's a valuable lesson here. A lot of people get up in the morning, jump in the car, and go to a job they don't really care for because it pays the bills. At the end of the day, they get back in their car, fight traffic to get home, eat dinner, and go to bed—only to wake up a few hours later and do it all over again.

If you're like me, you need more than that. Being alive and simply existing aren't necessarily the same thing. This doesn't mean I neglect my responsibilities or quit my job. But it does mean I pursued a career and take on responsibilities that allow me to enjoy doing what I love. Everything about being outside in nature makes me feel alive, and the ability to include my wife and kids in this passion fills me up. Hiking, hunting, exploring, and taking the time to do something as simple as watching the sunset all energize me.

My journey isn't about reaching the top of the mountain—it's about all the wonderful things I get to see while climbing.

Honestly, I have no idea where my path is leading. I didn't set out to build a television show or write a book. I started as a guy who loved the outdoors and wanted to share that love with others. Somewhere along the way, God decided to open all the right doors for my family and me, but it began simply as a desire and an unwavering commitment to do more than just exist.

Do you believe that God created you for more than simple existence? That you were put here for something beyond being born, bearing life's burdens, and then dying? You get only one life on this earth, so do the things you've only been talking about. What you keep putting off is not likely to happen on its own. Take some chances and don't be afraid.

For most of my life, I've felt like the guy who always gets the short end of the stick. If you've watched *Raised Hunting*, I bet you had no idea that in the past, I often wondered why I seemed to have a black cloud hanging over me. Does that surprise you?

I've always been the guy who never won anything. To this day, if Karin and I both enter a drawing, she can put in a single ticket and win a gun. I can put in 500 tickets and not win anything! I've often thought I was doing something wrong, because no one has luck this bad. When I worked at the fire department, a battalion chief was secretly sabotaging my career. He even made sure I worked on Christmas day—four years in a row! Even though I made captain the day after I was eligible, he constantly fought against me.

Now that I've been able to sit back and look at my life from a different perspective, I realize that life didn't give me the short end of the stick. Instead, God was making me into the person He wanted me to be by giving me challenges to overcome. I used to complain a lot and even disagree with God about the circumstances of my life. Now I no longer complain, because I can see that God is taking me somewhere.

When Karin and I were dating, I went on and on about wanting to see a record-book deer, since I had never seen or killed one. But at this moment, my new office is being measured for a trophy room. Soon I will hang more than 40 deer mounts in that space—and many of them qualify for the record books.

God is making up to me all the times I felt cheated. I think it's partly because I'm no longer focused on what I don't have and am instead thanking God every day for what I do have. I owe God so much. He stuck with me when I didn't care enough or take the time to be thankful.

If you believe you always get the short end of the stick, think about being nailed to a cross. Imagine being a perfect person trying to share a perfect message, but no one cares. That was Jesus. That's the short end of the stick.

I can speak only for myself, but I don't have any room to complain when I compare my life to my Savior's. If I died today, God will have still given me far more than I deserve.

If you believe life is a black cloud, I challenge you to look around. I'm betting you have more than you think. I just wrote the narration for a show we're doing for a 15-year-old named Austin, who has leukemia. He is fighting to stay alive so he can go on one more hunt. Put yourself in his shoes for one day. I'm guessing your life isn't so bad. Admit it, dig deep, and take note of the many ways God has blessed you.

KARIN | On this hunt, the antelope responded to Warren and Easton's cow trick exactly the way we were hoping, but it isn't always that way in life. Sometimes you put in the work only to get something you weren't expecting.

In 2008, I was working for Edward Jones Investments. During this time, we experienced the largest drop in the stock market since the Great Depression. I was battling the emotions of my clients (as well as my own) every day. The Dow was going down fast, not to mention the value of homes, land, gold, silver, and bonds. Anything with a dollar sign attached to it was losing value. Many brokers were hiding under their desks and not calling clients, but I began at the top of my list and called until I got through to all of them. Then I went back to the top and started all over again. I did this for two years straight. My clients were begging to sell their investments, to essentially commit financial suicide. I told them to stay focused on the long term because "this too shall pass." And it did.

This is the part of life that can become confusing. You think if you put in the effort, it should all work out, right? In my lifetime, I have found that's not always true. Sometimes things happen that you never bargained for. What then? Do you quit, lose hope, pout, or throw a fit? Whenever I've tried those options, nothing got resolved. I'm learning to think about life not in terms of what I'm getting but with regard to what I'm giving. My goal is to positively impact the lives of as many people as possible and to make sure I'm working every day toward reaching that goal.

I believe we are all designed for this purpose. By investing time and resources into others, I'm really investing in myself. For example, I love to invest in and spend quality time with my boys. I'm not on the sidelines of life, simply cheering them on. I'm in the game, participating with them.

For instance, when we are hunting together, we're working toward accomplishing a goal: harvesting an animal that will feed our family. We spend a lot of time in a tree stand, where we might not see a deer all day. However, I get to spend eight hours in a tree with my son with no distractions. You can learn a lot from this time spent together. I had to find a way to create those moments with Warren and Easton. I value those experiences with my boys and treasure them above all else. If we're hunting, shooting, exercising, or just hanging out in the outdoors, my life feels full regardless of what might not go as planned.

DAVID | To get the most out of life, eventually you must take an honest look at your relationship with God and go all in. For years, God didn't have all of me, but He does now. I no longer pray just to get another sponsor or beg God for a bigger buck. That's the old David. The new David makes time every single day to talk openly and honestly with Jesus. If I can tell Him what He already knows, my day goes better! For me, prayer is bouncing my thoughts off a God who has already put the answers inside me. I just need to follow His lead.

I love to hunt so much because that's where I feel most connected to God. There is something about it that makes me feel alive—besides the fact that I love animals. You may be surprised to hear me say I love animals, especially if you don't hunt. The truth is, aside from people, I respect animals more than anything else on the planet. I want to understand the animals I hunt. I want to help them thrive. Animals don't judge me, make me feel bad about myself, or hurt my feelings. Animals are a renewable resource, given to us by God. We should celebrate the fact that He has trusted us with them by using ethical means to hunt them.

Whether I'm in church or in a deer stand, God has all of me. I used to question the importance of complete surrender to God, but I now realize my life depends on it. I'm not going to lie: I sometimes feel like one of those 12 crazy guys Jesus found to share His message. I'm the kind of guy people scratch their heads and question God about: "Why did you pick *him*? He's not a very good representative."

I'm not sure why God lets me speak for Him, but I'm honored and grateful that He does. I don't feel qualified to quote Scripture, but I do understand some of it as I read and study. I understand what God is saying to me when my pastor is teaching. I'm working to recognize God's voice and notice when He is leading me into something new. There are certain things in life that are worth any cost. My relationship with God is one of those things.

KARIN | Lately, I've been on a more personal journey in my relationship with God. I'm hungry for something intimate and unique to me. I'm completely aware of the fact that God and I are on this journey together. Unlike with hunting, I can't depend on my husband or sons for success. This one is on me. I'm learning that time spent getting to know God fills the empty places in my life. (Yes, I do have empty places.) I'm realizing that for me, I will be completely fulfilled when I have a deep and intimate knowledge of who God is.

Coming from the financial world, I'm aware of the importance of investment. My clients cannot withdraw from accounts without first making investments. I like to think of my relationship with God the same way: The more I invest my time in Him, the stronger my foundation becomes. The more truth I know and understand, the more I can draw from it when life feels out of control.

A life devoted to things is a dead life, a stump;
a God-shaped life is a flourishing tree.
PROVERBS 11:28 MSG

ANCHOR POINTS

- What you get out of life and hunting is completely up to you.
- Time spent teaching your kids is also time spent *with* your kids.
- Being alive is more than just existing. Find what energizes you and make decisions that allow you to enjoy doing what you love.
- Make sure to *do* the things you've only been talking about.
- To get the most out of life, you must take an honest look at your relationship with God and go all in.

CONFESSION FIRE

What makes you feel alive? What decisions will you make so you can enjoy what you love?

KARIN'S GAME PLAN

ITALIAN ELK SAUSAGE PIZZA

INGREDIENTS

4 oz. Italian elk sausage
1 16-gram Protein Golden Home ultrathin pizza crust
¼ cup Colby Jack cheese (shredded)
2 T. low-sodium tomato paste

DIRECTIONS

1. Preheat oven to 375 degrees.

2. Brown the Italian elk sausage.

3. Spread the tomato paste on the pizza crust.

4. Layer the elk sausage across the entire crust.

5. Sprinkle the shredded cheese on top.

6. Bake for 10 to 12 minutes or until golden brown and cheese is melted.

NUTRITION

Serving size—2 slices (½ of pizza)
Calories—180
Fat—5.2 grams
Carbohydrates—7.5 grams
Protein—24.5 grams

9

DIRT

Dream Big

DAVID | Karin has always been a "go big or go home" person. That's just one of the many reasons I love her so much. In chapter 6, she shared an adventure we had on the side of a mountain in Montana while scouting for moose and battling thunderstorms. We returned a few days later during moose season. This is the story of Karin's first archery kill.

It's not easy to draw a moose tag in Montana. In fact, it can take years, but as I've mentioned, Karin seems to have the best of luck. This hunt was no exception—she drew a cow moose tag on her first try. The plan was to spend four days in the mountains. As we were packing the truck and preparing to leave, I found a heavy yellow rope behind the seat. It had been there a while, but I had never needed to use it. Believing I wouldn't need it on this trip, I took it out.

After a five-hour drive, we were getting close to our camping spot. Turning onto the gravel road, Karin looked out the driver's side window and spotted a giant cow moose standing in a perfect spot for a stalk. Typically, we find our spot and set up camp before we even come close to finding whatever we're planning to hunt. Finding this moose caught us off guard.

We parked the truck and bailed out. Back then, camouflage wasn't as good as it is today. Karin was wearing an army-green jacket, so we had to move very slowly to avoid being seen by the moose. Karin was so excited that she put her quiver on upside down. To this day, I still don't know how she did it! Looking over at her, I had to laugh as her arrow fletchings pointed toward the sky.

We were forced to crawl on our hands and knees through the willows. To complicate the situation even more, this was my first time trying to film while stalking prey. I had filmed only one other deer kill, and that was nothing compared to this.

Once at the creek, Karin rose up to get a better look. "There it is," she whispered. We were within 20 yards, and to my surprise, the moose lay down. Now it was a waiting game. The wind was in our favor. The moose had no idea we were there. Karin was up on a little mound of dirt, and I was behind her. The plan was to let the moose stand up, and once Karin came to full draw, I'd step up next to her and film the kill.

Fifteen minutes passed. Karin turned and looked at me. "It's up," she said. I turned on the camera, but Karin was already at full draw. I couldn't see the moose, so I just held the camera over my head and aimed it in the general direction her bow was pointed. I'll never forget the look on her face as she let that arrow fly. She watched with one hand covering her mouth. Her eyes were huge as the cow teetered. "I think I got it!" she said.

I wasn't sure.

We didn't see the moose fall, instead watching as she suddenly disappeared into the brush. Karin was sure she had hit it, but I still wasn't convinced. To get across the creek, we had to make a 45-minute circle around to where the moose should be lying. As we topped a little knoll, we could see the moose, already down. Even stretched out on its side, it was so big that it came up past Karin's hip! I couldn't believe what had just happened, and I was shocked at how giant this moose really was.

The temperature was in the seventies that day, and I knew we had to get the moose out quickly before the meat spoiled. But how? It was a 45-minute trip back to the truck. Then I had the bright idea of trying to get the moose out whole. I could tie a rope to the back of the truck and drag the carcass through the creek. After all, I had been carting around

Karin's dream is realized when she harvests this great buck on her own land.

a big yellow rope in my truck forever. Oh, wait—I had removed the rope. All I had was a small cord that was 75 yards too short.

It took some convincing, but Karin finally agreed to help drag the 750-pound moose to the rope. Somehow, we managed to pull the moose, an inch at a time, to the edge of the creek where the rope was. I tied the cord to the moose and then to the front of the truck. Karin got behind the wheel and tried to back up, but the moose's shoulders got caught in the brush along the creek bank. Fearing the rope would break, I had one option. We rolled the moose onto its back, and I crawled underneath it. As Karin inched backward in the truck, I bench-pressed the moose, freeing it from the brush. As crazy as it sounds, it worked, and we successfully dragged the moose across the creek.

Our next problem was hoisting the moose into the truck. As we stood there, wondering how to proceed, I saw headlights. A hunter we had seen earlier, parked at the end of the road, was now returning. He helped us load up the moose. After packing it in ice, we drove the five hours back home. We have a picture of Warren with one of the hooves, which was bigger than his head! That was the start of Karin's archery career. She's been hooked ever since!

ON THE HUNT

Most of us have been there: You scout, plan, and maybe even hang a tree stand or two, only to arrive on opening morning of deer season and find someone else already sitting in the exact spot you planned to hunt. That's what happened to Warren and me in 2004. As we were scrambling in the dark, trying to find another place to sit, I made him a promise: "One day I'll change this. We'll have our own land to hunt."

Occasionally, you'll find yourself chasing more than an animal. When this happens, the passion inside you will rise up and cause you to go after whatever you want most. Roadblocks will always block your path, but you must go through them to reach your goals. For me, the dream of owning a piece of land began long before my boys were born. But by the time they were old enough to hunt, the dream had become a need. As I waited for it to become a reality, at times the dream felt more like a nightmare. There was no answer in sight. The passion was simple; fulfilling it wasn't. I constantly asked myself, *Why is it so hard to buy some dirt?*

In 2014, my hope to own land was finally within reach. After hitting several dead ends, I eventually found 80 acres with timber, water, and areas of grass perfect for whitetail deer to bed in. It bordered agriculture, which in Iowa is the key to growing big bucks. Karin was just as excited as I was. "We've been saving for this," she said. "Let's put in an offer."

Ten years earlier, I had made a promise to my son, and ten years before that I had made a promise to myself. Our offer was accepted, and as Karin and I signed the contract, I made good on that promise. I can't explain how incredible it felt. We finally owned our own piece of dirt—piece of heaven, if you ask me. We didn't feel that we were signing our lives away, but rather that life was signing us up for what we had been dreaming about.

I'm a hunter, husband, and dad. I'm also a dedicated Christian, but on that day, for the first time in my life, I was a landowner. As I opened the red gate leading into the property, I couldn't help but feel both overwhelmed and thankful.

The four of us went to work clearing brush and planting food plots. This dream, like most, came with a to-do list. Buying the property was just the first step. Preparing it for hunting season felt like a marathon. We all have dreams. Some of us hang on to them while others allow them to slip away. My dream of owning land was about more than just me; it was just as much about my wife and sons. Sharing my dream with them was what made it so special. For the Holders, the power of breathing life into a plan creates the best memories, and when we're all working together…those are the best moments. We set out to have a place to hunt, but what we got was the satisfaction of knowing that what we do together as a family means more to us than any piece of ground. The new land was special—and not just because the food plots came up quickly or because we knew there were big bucks in the area. It was special because we would now enjoy it as a family.

Bow season that year felt different from others. As Easton and I left the house early on a Saturday morning, we talked about how I had waited my entire life to hunt on my own piece of property and about the promise I'd made to Warren years earlier. Easton was 14 at the time and had no way of knowing how his 47-year-old dad was feeling. Looking back, it's hard to put into words. All I knew was that topping the hill, crossing the creek, and climbing into a tree on ground that I owned was something I had done only inside my head until that day. As we settled into the tree stand, it all began to sink in. I was living the dream. Even though we didn't fill a tag that day, my heart still felt full.

Our next trip to the same stand had a different ending. "I see a really big buck, and he's heading this way," Easton said. "I've got the camera on him. You just shoot." The giant whitetail jumped the fence and quickly closed the gap between us. I was nervous and felt like I was going to throw up at any second! This was the moment I had been waiting for, the opportunity to take a deer on land we owned. Somehow I came to full draw, and once the deer stopped, I released the arrow.

Easton and I watched him go down not far from where we were. As we sat and waited, giving the buck ample time to pass, I couldn't help but reflect on the long journey it had taken to get there. We didn't own a lot of land by some people's standards, but the land was ours, and we had worked hard for it. Even though I had already killed more animals with my bow than I could count, this one meant more. Why? Because this deer was the one I had waited for my entire life. As we approached the buck, I saw that he was even bigger than I first thought. But it wasn't his size that mattered to me that day. What mattered most was that the dream was now complete. We had bought the property, planted the food plots, and prayed to the good Lord for success. He had given us that and then some.

That day was about dirt and a family's quest to own a piece of it. But in all the journeys we've been on, I realize there is one story we still haven't told. The story of what you, the reader, mean to us. You see, we set out to write a book about hunting, but this has become so much more. We aren't just writing a book; we are building a bond between you and us. We are *Raised Hunting*, and so are you. You are our family.

BEYOND THE HUNT

Honestly, I still struggle with being patient. You can probably imagine how difficult it was for me to wait so long to buy those 80 acres. Wanting something so bad and not being able to make it happen can be agonizing, I think because it's just human nature to want to arrive at your goals as quickly as possible. But what if God's goal for your life includes more than just getting you there? I've come to realize that God's main priority isn't hand-delivering to me everything I want on a silver platter. I believe He wants me to achieve my dreams, but more than that, I believe He wants me to be the person He created me to be. He wants me to grow into the person I'm supposed to be along the way. That can take time.

I sometimes get frustrated when I have to reteach Warren and Easton something I've already taught them, believing they should have paid more attention the first time. I wonder if God gets equally frustrated with me when He has to teach me the same lesson over and over because *I'm* the one not paying close attention. God gives us what we're ready for when we're ready for it. If He gave it to us too soon, we probably wouldn't have what it takes to keep it.

I'm always shooting for goals and dreams. But I don't just sit around hoping that maybe, someday, I might get my wish. While I'm waiting, I can do proactive things to partner with God in fulfilling a new dream. I don't have a magic formula, but I have discovered some actions to take and actions to avoid when I feel as if I'm not gaining ground.

1. What can I do to fill the space I'm in? Once you learn to occupy the space you're in, waiting becomes easier. For instance, we don't always get to go every place we want to hunt, and occasionally the door closes on land we've previously hunted. That happened to us recently on a farm in Montana where previously we hunted for antelope. When that door closed, we

Warren Holder at age 5, already a super fan of hunting. In the background is the Holders' dog Arson.

decided the best use of our time wasn't to be upset, but to simply find another place to hunt, which we did. As it turned out, the new place was much better than the old place. We even met some people who will surely become lifelong friends. When we filled the space we were in, God took us forward to places we had never been! Make the most of where you are right now.

2. Leave the timing to God. As I write this part of the chapter, we just received word that one of the publishers we were hoping would make an offer to publish this book declined. Even though we were ready to move forward, God wasn't ready yet. In the past, I might have been upset by that kind of disappointment. I've been known to tell God what He needs to do and when He needs to do it. But a few years ago, I realized that doesn't work, and even though I still struggle a little with letting God guide the future, I know He can do a better job than I can.

3. Realize the tough stuff in life is there not to upset you, but to teach you.

Karin and I had to learn the hard way. When we began *Raised Hunting*, there was no one to show us what to do or what not to do. It was the school of hard knocks all the way.

I started as a pro staffer for Primos Hunting, and even though I loved doing it, I didn't get paid. We had to work our way through the tough stuff, and now we have a top television show in the outdoor industry. With God's help, we persevered through difficulty, and we found that our hardest lessons caused our greatest opportunities. When life feels difficult, use that to fuel the dream inside you. On days when you feel like quitting, remember why you started in the first place.

KARIN | I'll be the first to admit I've been more than blessed in this life. God has given me too many wonderful things to count, and I would include you on that list! I'm grateful for every single person who has taken this crazy journey with us. As you read this book, I want you to know how much I value and appreciate you. Together, we are all *Raised Hunting*.

Many of my dreams have already come true, and thankfully, David and I shared the same dream of owning land. We had to take some risks and work extremely hard to see that dream fulfilled, but it was worth the sacrifice. For us, staying focused and concentrating on the action steps necessary to get where we are were key. If we had allowed distractions to overtake us or had settled for less than what we were looking for, the dream could have easily been compromised or even lost.

Even though I have worked in the corporate world for 20 years, I've always felt my place was in the country, and I'm proof you can have both. You can be a career woman and find your own little piece of heaven in nature too if that's what you want.

I was also tired of knocking on doors to try to find a place to hunt, of driving for hours to hunt a piece of ground, only to arrive and find someone else already hunting there. I wanted a place where I could experience wildlife in my backyard. I wanted my dog to be able to run without fences and boundaries. I wanted a big blue sky in the day and a night sky full of stars to call my own. We have all that with our piece of dirt. That might not sound like a lot to some, but to me, it is everything.

I believe you can have more than one dream. As you grow, develop, and have life experiences, you evolve and change. When this happens, don't be alarmed—God created you to always be reaching for more. My dreams certainly have changed over time. I currently have a dream of impacting the lives of one million women. My dream is to help them understand their value, believe in themselves, and have the confidence to do anything they want. That dream is a big part of why we decided to write this book. My prayer is that you will learn from my mistakes and success.

Karin Holder with Old Dan, one of the many reasons she says, "I've been more than blessed in this life."

When David and I set out to get our own land, we had nothing—and by nothing, I mean no money. We saved and worked long, hard hours just to have enough for a down payment. If you had asked me 20 years ago if I would own ground in Iowa, I would have thought the idea was crazy. But here we are, living that dream because God provided the path we needed to accomplish our goal.

My dream to help women sometimes feels like it's on the back burner while David and I work on other dreams God has placed in our hearts. In the meantime, however, I'll continue to journal about why I want to help women, how I want to help them become all they dream of, and how they in turn can help other women. Having this dream but being unable to act on it immediately is extremely challenging at times. But I believe God will let me know when the time is right. If you have a dream that's not yet realized, rest assured that God is timing things perfectly for you as well.

DAVID | Your dream matters to God. After all, He is the one who gave it to you. It can be difficult to trust God's timing and push through the hard stuff while you're waiting for your turn. For years, I lived with the philosophy that if you wanted something, you went after it, and if you got it, good for you. I believed that life just kind of randomly gave me success based on my own efforts. I had this false notion that success was completely up to me.

I never felt as if God had forgotten me or didn't care, but I did think life was more about what I was doing and less about what He could do. That was the old David. The new David understands that dreams come from God and that He wants to partner with me in reaching them. Realizing this has taken me years. Perhaps you can relate to my story.

As hard as it is for me to admit, there was a time when I felt like God was holding me back because I wasn't good enough. I honestly believed He was punishing me for not serving Him the right way. I will use *Raised Hunting* as an example. I love our television show, but it's never been an easy path. There are constant challenges. At times, we've wondered if it's worth the strain and stress it puts on our family. We deal with everything from hunts that don't go as planned to sponsors who aren't always satisfied.

For years, I was the guy who said, "Come on, God, why are You making this so hard? Can't You give me a break?" I couldn't see how overcoming the obstacle in front of me was making me a better hunter, not to mention a way better person. God had my dream in mind, but all I had in mind was the bad I was seeing. Yet God knew where He was taking me and what I needed to learn before I could get there.

Thankfully, Karin and I have both learned to put our lives and our show in God's hands. Because of the struggles we share through the show, we get emails all the time from people who are facing the same tough situations that we have been through—or much worse. If we hadn't faced those challenges and overcome them, we would be just another hunting show. Our dream to be *more* has led us to trust God more. That's a very good thing in my book.

I get it now. God isn't looking to get even with me for all the times I should have trusted Him and not doubted. No—He is asking me to follow Him and believe He is in control. I imagine He is asking the same of you.

I still have days when doubt tries to creep in, but I have to remember that what I'm trying to accomplish and what God is trying to teach me might not always look the same.

If you're feeling cheated, please know that God has not forgotten you. Your dreams and goals are just as important to Him as they are to you. He is laying the groundwork in His own time. You don't have to figure it out; God is simply asking for your cooperation and patience. God never leaves us, even if we can leave Him. And when we do, we might not even realize that we are back on our own again. But you don't have to leave God to doubt or ask why; just believe and trust. Put your faith in the One who gave you that dream in the first place. Let Him know that you're okay with Him being in control. When I stop worrying, my stress level goes down, and my life just feels better. I can accomplish so much more in His time than I ever could in mine, and the same will be true for you.

KARIN | I truly believe God has plans for each of us. You were designed for a reason and for His purpose. God wants the best for you. You have a dream for your life, and so does God. The hard part is connecting to God's dream for the future when you don't have all the information. Your journey through this life, as well as the things you experience (both good and bad), are all shaping your dream. Your character will be tested and developed as you get closer to accomplishing your goal. It should come as no surprise that things often get more difficult before getting easier.

Let's look at this from another perspective. What if you have no clue what direction your life is supposed to take, and feel as if you're just wandering aimlessly? My best advice is for you to sit down and begin to think about what makes you truly happy. Is there something stirring inside you that you haven't yet given yourself permission to think about because it seems so far out of reach? If so, that's exactly the kind of stuff dreams are made of! When you dig deep into yourself, get past the protective barrier, drop the facade of who you think you should be, and peel back the layers—that's when you find out who you really are.

There's a dream inside you trying to get out. Like a seed planted too far beneath the dirt, that dream will die if you don't begin uncovering it. One of the saddest things in life is to see someone never live up to their full potential and die without really knowing what they could have done.

If you're having trouble identifying why God put you here, consider the following questions and use the Confession Fire portion of this chapter to write your responses.

- What do you value?
- What are you doing when you are having the most fun?
- What activities make you feel fully alive?
- What is holding you back from being your true self in front of others?
- What are you passionate about?
- In what area of your life do you most want to make a difference?

After you've been radically honest with yourself concerning each of these questions, consider your responses and pay attention for a common theme. I bet your dream will come rising to the top! Now ask God to reveal to you how to make that dream come true.

This vision is for the future time. It describes the end, and it will be fulfilled. If it seems slow in coming, wait patiently, for it will surely take place. It will not be delayed.
HABAKKUK 2:3 NLT

ANCHOR POINTS

- Life can feel like a nightmare when you're waiting for a dream to come true. Dream anyway.

- God gives us what we're ready for because if He gave it to us too soon, we might not appreciate it or even keep it.

- The tough stuff in life is there not to upset you but to teach you.

- As you work toward accomplishing your goal, God will provide the path.

CONFESSION FIRE

Consider the questions Karin posed at the end of this chapter and use them to help you identify your dream.

KARIN'S GAME PLAN

GRILLED TURKEY BREAST

INGREDIENTS

1 turkey breast
½ cup soy sauce
½ cup teriyaki sauce
½ cup Worcestershire sauce

DIRECTIONS

1. Cut the turkey breast into thin strips and place it in a 1-gallon ziplock bag.

2. Add the sauces or your own creation to the bag.

3. Shake the bag so all the turkey is covered.

4. Let the meat marinate for 24 to 48 hours in the fridge.

5. Remove the pieces and place on a grill.

6. Rotate every 2 to 3 minutes to keep them from burning.

NUTRITION

Serving size—3½ oz.
Calories—163
Fat—1 gram
Carbohydrates—0
Protein—26 grams

10

KARIN'S QUEST

Failing Forward

DAVID | We all have our own way of processing failure. Some see failure as a red light and quit, while others learn from it and wait for the next green light, believing the slowdown was temporary. I've spent nearly three decades with Karin, and one thing I know for sure is that she always fails forward. In other words, she learns from her mistakes and moves past them. As I think back to the beginning of our relationship, it's always been that way.

When Karin and I began dating, she had very little hunting experience. The men in her family hunted, but she was never invited to join them. So I invited her. The plan was to go on a squirrel hunt, but Karin had never fired a shotgun. She asked me to teach her how. That was when things took a turn for the worse. Instead of properly positioning her to shoot a shotgun—standing, feet apart, and with the stock of the gun firmly pressed to her shoulder to avoid kickback—I placed my 12-gauge on a sandbag, as you would to sight in a rifle. When Karin pulled the trigger, the gun jumped up and smacked her in the nose! Immediately, blood gushed. I felt horrible, but thankfully she didn't hate me enough to leave.

To my surprise, a couple of weeks later Karin still wanted to hunt squirrels with me. She was even willing to try the shotgun again. In Virginia, squirrels are plentiful. I've always enjoyed hunting and eating them. Rainy days are best in my opinion, so after a hard rain, we went on Karin's first official hunting trip. I took her behind the gun range where I had made my first real bow kill. We were walking through the timber about 40 yards apart when I heard her shoot. I saw the squirrel fall out of the tree and hit the ground. I was thrilled for Karin and went over to congratulate her. To this day, I still remember every detail of what happened next.

Karin turned around and looked at me. Keep in mind those 1980s hairstyles. She had long, permed hair with curled bangs. Tears were streaming down her face. At first, I thought the gun had kicked her again, but then she said, "He's still breathing." I looked down. Sure enough, the squirrel wasn't dead. My initial thought was, *Oh no, she's never going to hunt again.* I finished the job and picked up the squirrel and put it in my pocket so she wouldn't have to look at it. Believing she was "over" hunting squirrels, I asked what she wanted to do next. Karin wanted to keep hunting.

A few minutes later, I heard another loud boom. Again, Karin had taken a shot, and another squirrel fell to the ground. I pictured her reacting the same way she had to her first squirrel, so I was prepared to go back over there and console her once more. I started walking toward her, but before I could get there, I saw her reach down, pick up the squirrel, and put it in her pocket! She didn't even turn around to see what I was doing. I stood still and said, "Heck yeah! Check that out!" That was the moment I knew Karin was the one for me. She was not only beautiful but also unafraid to shove a dead squirrel in her pocket!

That night we built a fire and roasted the squirrels whole over the coals. Karin said, "This looks horrible but tastes fantastic!" I learned a lot about her on that squirrel hunting trip, and to this day she is the same woman. She wins some and she learns some. That's Karin Holder.

ON THE HUNT

When you marry, you take vows; when you have kids, you take pride; when you walk, you take a journey; and when you stumble, you

As a financial advisor, Karin helps people reach their financial targets and a different kind of target as well.

get up. When you see, you take it in, and when you have wronged, you apologize. Life is a series of give-and-takes. Anyone who meets Karin quickly learns that failure is not an option for her. When she faces a seemingly impossible challenge, she takes it on, giving her very best. She believes if you learned something, you didn't really fail; you just figured out what doesn't work. That's her give-and-take.

Karin's quest to kill an elk began in 2011. At first, we chalked up all the missed opportunities as part of the territory: "That's just elk hunting." Unfortunately for her, it appeared to be more than just setting up in the wrong spot, a sudden change in wind direction, or being busted because there wasn't enough cover to conceal our location. What began as a typical bow hunt for a bull elk became a lesson in what to do when nothing you're doing seems to be working. As the 2011 season ended, Karin was frustrated yet remained optimistic. She thought next year would no doubt be her year.

In 2012 and 2013, bulls came and went. On paper, every plan she and I came up with was perfect. But every time we got close, it seemed like we were getting further away from accomplishing our goal. We were trying everything in our power to get her that elk—every tip, trick, and tactic. But no matter what we did, it wasn't enough. We tried new places and new approaches. We went out earlier and stayed later. When that didn't work, we drove farther and hiked deeper. Even then, it seemed like we just couldn't catch a break.

An unwritten rule says that when you shoot an animal with a bow, you should wait at least 30 or 40 minutes before tracking it. This keeps you from jumping a wounded animal and possibly losing it forever. If the shot is lethal, doing this will allow the animal to pass in peace.

In the context of a lifetime, 40 minutes can go by in the blink of an eye. But for a hunter, the few minutes that pass after an arrow has found its mark can feel like an eternity. The time can pass so slowly you can almost feel it ticking, just as you can feel the pulse in your own veins. Here in those 40 minutes, the memories of past places, sights, and sounds flood your thoughts. This was the place Karin was working toward, even though everything was working against her. If she could get in position to release an arrow, all the time invested would no longer matter.

As life rolled by, so did the encounters, seasons, miles, and frustration. Elk hunting tested Karin's drive more than any hunter's I've ever witnessed. But with every obstacle, she maintained hope, and she faced every issue that arose like a champ. She never wavered in her quest.

At 7:09 p.m. on Monday, September 29, 2014, everything finally seemed to come together exactly the way we had hoped. A giant bull elk came into bow range—36 yards. But the expression on Karin's face broke my heart as we watched the bull of a lifetime run away with her arrow stuck firmly in front of his back leg. This time Karin had missed her mark. After four days searching from the ground and one day searching from a small plane, we found nothing—no blood, no birds, and no hope. I did believe the elk was dead, but the country was so big that we had no way of knowing where he went.

When you hunt, you test yourself, taking life to a whole new level. Hunting provides rewards that are beyond description, but it also requires you to take a great risk, and when you take that risk, you're opening the door to great pain and disappointment. At *Raised Hunting*, we believe the reward for a well-executed hunt far outweighs the risk of those moments you wish you could take back. Karin couldn't take back her shot, but she could learn from it and keep shooting. The real question was, would she?

"I'm done, David," she said. "I'm sick. I can't do that again. The animal deserves more."

I did what any husband would do. I tried to be supportive and reassure her that she did nothing wrong. "Don't quit hunting because of one bad shot. Believe me when I tell you that every hunter has a story just like yours." I knew how Karin felt because I had been there.

They say time can heal all wounds, but what they don't tell you is that it can also reopen them. Six months later, we received a phone call: The landowner's son had found Karin's elk, but he refused to give up the elk's massive rack. This only added insult to Karin's injury, and I wasn't sure if she would get back in the game no matter how much I encouraged her to. One bad shot had led to an even worse situation. Even though the bull had been found, for Karin, the bull was now lost forever.

After receiving an encouraging e-mail from one of our *Raised Hunting* viewers, Karin agreed to give elk hunting one more try. After years of failure, missed opportunities, and utter heartbreak, she now had the resolve to close the door on her past failure. It was time to move on. I believe that God never gives you more than you can handle, but only He knows how much that is. Even when you think you can't take any more, He'll let you go just a little bit further. He might even let you go until you hit rock bottom. If God allows you to get to a low point, it's because He wants you to remember that He was the one who provided the path back to the top.

This was no longer just a quest for an elk; it was a test of Karin's will, and she was fighting for every person who had ever fallen short. She knew if she could carry her burdens and disappointments, others could carry theirs as well. She could model that tenacity for those watching our show.

Redemption came in 2016. After setting up the camera behind a few cedar trees, I began to make cow calls. It wasn't long before a curious bull wandered into bow range. Now at full draw, with the bull standing broadside, Karin released her arrow. This time she didn't miss. I can only imagine the raw emotion that flooded her as she watched the elk run away. Her now six-year quest was down to the 40-minute wait, the one we hunters hope and pray for. It wasn't a blood trail that morning; it was more like a roadmap. But we followed every drop so she could savor every step. The journey had been more than long; the quest more than hard; but in the end, Karin had passed the test. It wasn't easy, and in my opinion, that's why the reward was beyond description. As Karin put her hands on her bull, she also put her hands on life at a whole new level. Here's how she summed it up:

> I was ready to give up on elk hunting. Then I remembered why I love to hunt in the first place: I love to be outdoors, and I love to be with my husband in God's creation. There's no way I could ever give this up. When I look back, I realize it was more than a quest. It was a question of who I am and what I'm made of. The only way you will find an answer to something this personal is to go on your own journey.

BEYOND THE HUNT

Sometimes when you release an arrow, all you can think about are the times you missed in the past. But when you know the angle and distance are right? When your anchor point seems solid? If everything is right, why do you worry? I think we worry because we're human and know that even when we try to do everything perfectly, sometimes things can go very wrong. Saying that Karin was devastated after not finding her elk would be an understatement. At that moment, she needed more than just words of encouragement from Warren, Easton, and me. I was worried she had reached the point of no return. I'm so thankful she didn't quit.

It's human nature to pull back when you experience something traumatic or difficult to get through. You want to recoil, walk away, and give up too early. Karin could have easily decided never to elk hunt again, and I really don't believe anyone would have blamed her. The entire difficult season was a good lesson for our boys as they watched their mother persevere through her frustration.

People around you will need a strong shoulder when they experience something devastating they weren't prepared for. You don't have to push them forward the way I'm sometimes guilty of doing. You just need to be there. Your presence is enough.

I want to clearly point out something else here. When we didn't immediately find Karin's first elk, we prayed and asked God to help us. He didn't. You could look at that and say God didn't answer our prayers. To be honest, at one time in my life, I would have been the guy saying that. I will even take it one step further and admit there was even a time when I would have thought God was paying Karin back for some infraction. I thought God answered our prayers when He owed us for something we'd done right. And I thought God *didn't* answer our prayers because He needed to even the score. Now I realize God doesn't work that way. He isn't looking to even the score. God wants only what's best for me. His desire is to help me make it through this life with as much success as possible.

There was a bigger picture coming together on that hunt, one larger than simply killing an elk—just as there is more to your picture than you can currently make out. You may not be able to see all the colors right now, but in God's timing, He'll reveal them to you. I have often felt that God must have left me because I didn't have the answers I wanted. I've also been guilty of wanting only what I thought was best for me in my current situation, but now I try to stop and ask God if something is happening for the benefit of someone else. Life doesn't always give you what you want or what makes sense at the time. You just have to believe that one day it will. God hasn't given up on you, so don't give up on Him.

KARIN | I've thought long and hard about my journey to finally take an elk. It almost feels impossible to put such deep emotion into words, but if I can pass along anything at all that will help you when you feel like you've come up short, I'm happy to share my quest.

"Devastated" may sound like a strong word for a hunting scenario. After all, we usually reserve that term for the things in life that can't be fixed. However, if you were following the story on *Raised Hunting*, you already know that I had spent years preparing and practicing for that opportunity. When I fell flat on my face, all the dreaming I had done no longer mattered because my heart was completely broken. I felt that I had let down not only myself but everyone else too. David, my boys, and the countless women I wanted to inspire had just witnessed my utter failure.

Have you ever had to look at someone and see the disappointment in their eyes because of something you did? I have. It's a horrible feeling. It can cause you to stop believing in yourself and lead to anger, resentment, and depression. You can get to the place where you want to hide yourself away and quit. That's the point I had come to. I wanted nothing to do with something that might cause me or my family more hurt.

At the time, I didn't want to risk making another mistake and bring more heartache to everyone, myself included.

But then what? Do I pull back and stop trying just because I'm afraid I might be a disappointment again? Yes, I had missed my mark that day on the bull elk. But if I had never even tried, if I had not gotten into the game to begin with or if I disqualified myself before I even gave it a chance, I would not be living at all. Missing the mark is a part of both hunting and life.

The other thing to remember is you're going to miss 100 percent of the shots you do not take. If I had quit, where would my personal growth have come from? I would be going through the motions of life but not really living up to the potential or purpose God has in His plan for me. When you try something, you have no guarantee you will hit your mark; you might miss it completely. But you must keep a larger picture in mind. Each miss takes you one step closer to the bull's-eye. Once you get there, you'll be glad you kept shooting.

DAVID | When circumstances go wrong around you, you don't have to go wrong too. God will always give you what you need when you need it. It has taken me a long time to figure out that God would rather walk me through the hard stuff than carry me through it. Don't get me wrong; sometimes life can be so overwhelming that you feel you can't take another step. In those times, God will pick you up and carry you out. I'm thankful He never leaves me in my trouble, but I believe I learn more about who I am—and who God is—when He helps me keep going instead of delivering me from the problem.

When life is weighing on me, God is the rock I lean on. The only thing God has ever asked from me is that I turn my struggles over to Him. A lot of people blame God when sadness walks into their lives. In Karin's case, she could have blamed God for not answering her prayers to find that first elk. After all, she did hit it, even though her shot placement was off. As devastated as she was, many things in this life are even more devastating. It can be hard to trust God with the future when you don't feel like He has helped you in the past. I don't claim to have all the answers here, but I do know that we all go through hard things. When you find yourself questioning whether God cares, remember that it's impossible for Him *to not* care. The trap is to mistake His silence for His absence.

Trusting God when life isn't going your way often includes forgiving those who may have contributed to your difficult situation. This hunt was made more difficult because once the elk was recovered, it was kept from Karin. Even though we still haven't given up on getting Karin's elk antlers back, we also don't let it ruin our lives. We may occasionally talk about how nice it would be to have that rack, but we don't dwell on why it's being kept from us. I've forgiven the person who has her antlers. I believe God will work on his heart until he returns them to her. In the same way, God will help you forgive others once you decide He alone has the power to deal with them. Maybe, like Karin on this hunt, you need to stop, regroup, and pay attention to the fact that God has been with you the entire time. God did not fail her, and He will not fail you.

KARIN | This may come as a surprise to you, but in my earlier years, I was a rebel who gave little thought to God. My father was a Marine, and our household was strict. But even if I was told no, I would do something anyway, just to prove I could. I was a challenge for my parents, to say the least. As a young woman in a Catholic household with a military father, I made a lot of poor decisions.

I met David when I was 13 years old. For the next four years, he hounded me to go out with him, but I held out until he finally wore me down. We started dating when I was 17, and I've been with him ever since. In the beginning, we made some poor choices. We moved in together, which in my family was a big no-no. I eventually stopped going to church. Going to church meant that I couldn't do the things I wanted to or keep living my lifestyle at the time, so I turned away and continued my downward spiral.

Perhaps you've been living below your Christian standards. You might be asking yourself why God would want you back and why He would forgive you. Could it be that you are so down on yourself that you don't want to look God in the eye and see His disappointment? I finally got to the point where I could no longer live with myself. I was tired of carrying the guilt and shame of my actions. I knew something had to change.

I'm here to encourage you, from the depths of my soul, to lift your eyes to God; He will be looking back at you with utter love. God's grace is far beyond our human ability to understand. You can confide your failures to Him without fear of rejection. He truly does want to help you fix any area of your life that is preventing you from hitting your mark. Let go, believe, and begin taking intentional action steps to get back on the right track.

For me, the first step was to acknowledge I had sinned and to ask God to forgive me. Then I had to face my parents and apologize for the way I had disrespected them. That was my step in the right direction. Now you take yours.

No matter how many times you trip them up, God-loyal people don't stay down long, soon they're up on their feet, while the wicked end up flat on their faces.

PROVERBS 24:16 MSG

ANCHOR POINTS

- You win some and you learn some.
- When things go wrong in life, don't go wrong with them.
- Each miss takes you one step closer to the bull's-eye, so keep shooting.
- No matter what you've done, God will forgive you.

CONFESSION FIRE

Failure is fatal only when you hang on to it instead of turning it over to God. Have you missed your mark? What are you willing to do about it?

KARIN'S GAME PLAN

SMOKED BACKSTRAP

INGREDIENTS

1 backstrap
several cloves garlic
olive oil
French bread (cubed)
thyme
garlic salt

DIRECTIONS

1. Rub down the backstrap the night before with your favorite seasonings. Then cover or wrap in foil before placing in the refrigerator.

2. Before smoking, slice slits into the backstrap and insert a garlic clove into each slit.

3. Rub the backstrap on both sides with olive oil.

4. Season the cubed French bread with the thyme and garlic salt. Toss it in olive oil and toast it.

5. Roll out the crumbs into a fine mixture before placing on top of the backstrap.

6. Wrap in aluminum foil.

7. Smoke 3 to 4 hours and then grill to desired doneness.

NUTRITION

Serving size—8 oz.
Calories—250
Fat—6 grams
Carbohydrates—0
Protein—43 grams

11

NO LIMITS

Enjoying Where God Has Placed You

DAVID | Every family has its own unique way of making decisions. I believe it's important to make those decisions together rather than one person deciding for everyone else how something is going to go. Karin and I have always tried to include each other in the decisions that affect our family. Now that our boys are getting older, we include them whenever possible. Sometimes, the challenging part is having the same goal but vastly different ideas about how to get there. Warren and Easton have their own ways of doing things, just as Karin and I have ours. None of us are necessarily wrong; we simply have different approaches to the things we care about. Of course, we're all pretty hardheaded, as I'm sure you have figured out.

So what do we do when we have the same purpose but don't agree on the method to achieve it? The truth is, we do what most families do—fight and argue! But even when things get heated, we sit down and listen to what the others are saying. The goal is to find some way of compromising so we each feel like our point of view matters. If we can put all our ideas into a workable plan, that's a good day in my book. I want my wife and boys to feel heard, supported, and cared for even if we can't agree. And I want to know they hear me too.

We're still finding new ways to listen to one another, be flexible, and

Trail camera photos like this one are an important tool for hunters.

work together. It's challenging at times, but in the end, we realize we get more accomplished when we pull together. We are a typical family. We love to hunt and we love each other, but we still have moments when we drive one another crazy and have to take everyone's feelings into consideration. Occasionally, someone gets angry or hurt when they don't get the result they were hoping for, but in the end, we always come back together and work through the difficulty. Yes, that takes time, but it also takes the pressure off any individual because we know we all support one another. If we rise or if we fall, we do it together. That is *Raised Hunting*. That is the Holder family.

ON THE HUNT

At the Holder house, deer seasons come and go, but the argument over which deer we're going to try to shoot remains the same. Karin and Easton are always ready to take down a good buck. I think that's why I enjoy hunting with them so much. If I'm in the woods with either, they are probably going to take a shot if the opportunity presents itself.

Warren, on the other hand, believes if you let a good buck live, he'll grow into a *great* buck. It's hard for me to take sides because Warren does have a point. However, like Karin and Easton, I have a hard time letting a nice deer walk away—especially when there's no guarantee something bigger will come along. Plus, there's always the chance that the one you let get away will wander onto someone else's land, and some other land-owner will get the buck you had decided to let grow for another season. If you've been deer hunting for long, you know exactly what I'm talking about. Do I shoot, or do I hold out for something better?

As we scrolled through trail camera photos one morning, Warren was picking out which deer we should shoot and which we should give more time to grow. His logic made sense, but he was setting limits for the rest of us. He was deciding for everyone else how the season was going to go before it had even started. Warren was measuring success by the size of the deer.

Regardless of what we do or how old we are, we each have our own way of measuring success. It's different for every one of us. A coach measures success by the number of wins; a kid by the number of friends. As deer hunters, we usually measure success by the amount of bone on an animal's head. At 18 years old, Warren was all about size that day, but this deer season he would learn that the point of deer hunting isn't always about how many points there are on a buck's head. Deer hunting is more…much more.

That evening, while bowhunting, Warren was still trying to manage our deer herd and telling Easton not to shoot at a wide eight-point buck. Luckily for Warren and the buck, Easton never had a clear shot. Karin and I, however, had managed to put ourselves in the perfect position for her to take the first buck of the season. A mature nine-point made his way down the trail. It would be his last trip, as Karin's arrow passed right through him. It was her second-largest deer ever with a bow, yet when I called Warren to tell him she had made a shot, all he wanted to know was, "How big?"

"It's as big as it's ever going to get," I said. "What does it matter any-way? Your mom is happy with it, so don't tell her what it scored. She doesn't care."

For Warren, the next two weeks brought nothing but time in the stand and encounters with deer he considered too small. No matter how hard we tried, Karin and I just couldn't get him to understand that there was more to deer season than merely the size of the antlers. Warren thought he was just having a streak of bad luck. We tried to convince him that deer hunting isn't about luck at all; it's about seeing the bigger picture that life is painting for us.

It seems the older my boys get, the harder it is for me to get through to them. In Warren's defense, he was 18. When I was that age, I didn't listen to my folks either.

Thank goodness life has a way of maturing us and showing us a better path. Warren was learning a hard lesson, and I, for one, was glad to see his mind starting to change. He still wanted to kill the biggest buck in the woods, but he was also beginning to realize that the size of the deer wasn't as important as enjoying the hunt itself. He was still frustrated, however, and it was the reason for his frustration that worried me. Warren grew up in an era when success had a measure, and for deer hunters, that measure was the number of points on a buck's head. The size of a kill mattered more than anything. Other hunters judged and ridiculed everything from what a person shot to how they shot it.

Don't get me wrong—Karin and I are grateful for the fact that our boys get to hunt with us on some of the best hunting ground anywhere, but this has also created its own problem. Without realizing it, Warren was having a season that most hunters would die for. He was regularly seeing plenty of really nice bucks, but because of his quest to kill the biggest and the best, he couldn't see the rest.

Thankfully, life has its own way of correcting you. When we parents just can't get through, life does. And when life teaches you a lesson, you don't forget it. I've found that life can change things overnight. Life can speed you up or slow you down. It can make you reflect on who you are, what you're doing, or where you're going. Warren and I are deer hunters, and like millions of others, if we were to tell you we didn't dream of big deer, we'd be lying.

I've reached that point in my hunting career where the hunt means more to me than the size of the antlers. This was a lesson Warren was still learning. And as much as I've tried to teach my boys to savor every deer encounter, I realize now that it's just one of those lessons you have to learn in your own time and in your own way. For Warren, that moment had finally arrived.

It was no longer about antler size or configuration—now, it was about having fun with his brother and delivering the most effective shot possible. That's all that should really matter to hunters. When the death of the animal occurs in less than 30 seconds, we should revel in the fact that we've done our job. In situations like these, we've all set our sights on something only to realize later that we were aiming at the wrong thing, forgetting that the real prize wasn't what we were after but where life took us to get there.

A patient hunter, Warren Holder once spent 18 all-day hunts before finding the "just right" buck.

Life had brought Warren back to the reality that just because you live in deer country and have big deer pictures, there are no guarantees that you will kill one. Life doesn't care what your deer scores.

After 18 all-day hunts, Warren finally took his buck. As I measured the horns, he said, "I don't care what he scores. I've never worked so hard for a deer in my life!" It was good to hear that Warren was listening while life was talking. For him, it was no longer all about the size of the deer but more about the size of the smiles. Warren's buck scored 109 inches—but then again, who's keeping score?

BEYOND THE HUNT

On this hunt, Warren had a picture in his mind of the result he wanted, but nothing went as he had planned. Hunting and life are similar in that regard—the results you get are rarely what you first envisioned. Just like Warren was waiting for a 180-inch deer, maybe you feel like you're waiting for your 180-inch life. It will be impossible for you to enjoy where God has put you now if you constantly compare what you're experiencing with what you were expecting. Only God knows the future, and He is taking you on a journey. It's important to learn to enjoy the quest.

You may find yourself struggling from time to time as to why you haven't arrived where you'd expected to. You might even believe God is punishing you for something you've done wrong in your past and think perhaps that's why you're not experiencing what you thought you'd have by now. As I've said many times, that was how I felt for years. That was David Holder, 100 percent.

Having grown up in a family that believed in God—but didn't really demonstrate that belief—I found it hard to understand who God was and how much He loved me in spite of my behavior. As a young man, I was headed down a dark road. By the time I was 15, I already drank heavily. I continued that lifestyle for years, not caring about anything but myself and what I was getting out of it. Hunting was the beginning of my journey out of a self-absorbed life. Hunting gave me something to enjoy that wasn't alcohol-driven or against the law.

For the first 23 years of my life, I was selfish, bullheaded, and destructive. Even after I started the journey to straighten up, I took a long time to figure out God wasn't holding those things against me. It's impossible to enjoy where you are in life when you constantly feel as if you owe God a debt you can't repay. The point is, you must forgive yourself for the things you regret and realize that God is not holding them over your head. God isn't in heaven looking down on you with a list of ten things you've done wrong and using them as an excuse not to answer your prayers. All God really wants from you is your dependence on Him. God wants you to recognize, worship, and love Him.

Now that I'm beginning to understand who God really is, my perspective has shifted from finding joy only in doing what I want to realizing that true joy and peace come by following God's will for my family and me. Once I made that transition in my mind, everything else began falling into place, including this book. I want you to experience this change as well. I encourage you to take a step back and look at your life. Is it really a disappointment, or does it just seem that way because you're still waiting for something big before you're willing to enjoy seemingly ordinary events?

Life can feel small when it's probably a lot bigger than you think. This hunt with Warren proves the point. What he thought wasn't much would have been everything to other hunters. When you feel as if life is coming up short, my advice is to quit trying to do it yourself and let God in. I fought with God over who would be in control for many years. In doing so, I wasted a lot of time. Regardless of whether things go as I've planned, I now enjoy where God has me right now.

KARIN | The grass is always greener on the other side. It's funny how cattle or horses are always sticking their heads through fences, trying to reach the few blades of fresh green grass at the tip of their reach. With heads cocked sideways and a strand of barbed wire stretched across their foreheads, they chomp on what they believe is worth all that effort. Occasionally, they strain so hard, they push completely through the fence and end up on the other side, wondering how they're going to get back in. They pull away from the herd because of a perceived advantage. Then they find themselves walking the fence line while trying to rejoin the group.

That analogy reminds me of our situation with Warren on this hunt. It's also a picture of life. When is enough, enough? At what point do you realize life isn't about sulking over what you don't have, but enjoying what you do have while waiting for what you want? A better question might be, Are you neglecting or even sacrificing any relationships or other elements of your life because you're pushing the limits so hard? And just like those horses and cattle, when you do reach the grass on the other side of the fence, will that really be enough to fill you up? My guess is no. That satisfaction, if it comes at all, will be short-lived. Then you'll need to push something else to the limit for an even higher high… and the vicious cycle starts all over. If I allow it to, life can become all about me, myself, and I.

This was the case with Warren and his search for a giant deer. In his defense, Warren wasn't asking everyone to hold off on a deer for his own personal gain. Instead, he had a long-term plan to help our farm grow bigger deer. He believes that if you always shoot the young bucks, you will never have the opportunity to shoot fully mature ones.

In this case, however, Warren wasn't considering that Easton was still a junior in high school and playing football. He did not have the time to fully commit to deer hunting. I have a full-time career and other businesses to run, so I do not have unlimited time either. For Easton and me, we needed to shoot what we could, not hold off.

There's a big difference between lasting joy and situational joy. If we had an opportunity to shoot something really big, how long would that joy last? To really enjoy life, you need to take a deep look inside and see what is truly important to you. What do you value? What do you believe at your core?

I learned this the hard way. When I first became a financial advisor, I was obsessed with being number one. I wanted to be the top producer at my level—anything less than that was failure. My goal was to make a lot of money. I did not want to have to worry about our financial future, and I wanted to help support our other dreams. I wanted the security and freedom that money could bring.

This put enormous strain on our family. I was seldom home and was often late for my boys' ball games. I was always at work, pushing the limits in order to achieve what I thought I needed to be happy and satisfied. I truly believed I was working hard for my family, but they thought they weren't as important to me as my career. And even though I disagreed, that was what I was demonstrating by my actions. Remember chapter 4, where I mentioned not feeling valued by my father because he never attended my events? Now I was doing the same thing to my boys. It was time for a change.

Even though I was achieving my goals, it wasn't enough. I still was not happy. This is when I realized my focus was on the wrong thing— I was focusing on numbers and production, but what I really wanted was to focus on my family and helping people. I wanted to leave people better off than when I found them, and that certainly included David and our boys. I had allowed myself to drift from them. I knew it was time to reevaluate my priorities so I could move closer. I needed a reality check, and that is exactly what I got! I took specific steps to address the situation, and you can too. If you've gotten a bit off track and lost sight of your priorities, consider the approach I took:

1. Make a list of the things you value most in life. God, family, career, heath, and so on. Once you've compiled a list of five or six items that are important to you, ask yourself, Which of these are getting the most attention, and which are getting none? Now that you've honestly evaluated your life, it's time to make the daily changes in your routine that will realign your actions with your values. Consider getting a journal and keeping track of where you're spending your time. Time is currency, and when you clearly see where you're spending it, you'll also see what you need to correct if you're serious about keeping the main thing the main thing.

2. Every day, identify three people you are thankful for. This is not optional. Express your gratitude out loud to at least one of those people every day. Thank them for being a part of your life. Tell them how grateful you feel to be taking the journey with them. You might even want to tell them how much you appreciate them for putting up with you when you're being hard to get along with. Trust me when I say this makes all the difference in the world to the people around you. No one ever gets tired of being appreciated.

3. Determine to look for lasting joy, not instant joy. I've found that lasting joy is usually tied to what I'm doing to help contribute to the lives of others, but instant joy is generally all about me and what I want at the time. I'm happiest when I'm adding to the lives of my family, friends, coworkers…and now you as part of the *Raised Hunting* family.

4. Read the Bible or a good daily devotional so you can learn to focus on what's important in God's eyes. Yes, I saved the best for last. My daily connection with God helps me stay focused on the things that really matter. Just spending a few minutes concentrating on God's Word creates a hunger inside me to not only be my best but also offer my best. There was no limit to how far Jesus was willing to go for me, and now I can return the favor by going all the way for Him. By doing this, I no longer feel the pressure of performing well for others. I just try to be as Christlike as possible. The rest takes care of itself.

DAVID | Warren was the only one setting limits for himself. He had created a small box full of self-imposed restrictions, but it didn't have to be that way. The rest of us were cheering for him, but for days his frustration only continued to build. He couldn't see the potential in himself that we saw in him. In the same way, what you see when you look at your life and what God sees may not always match. You may believe that God can't use you, that God is somehow limited by your mistakes. But He'll use the mistakes of your past to make you a better person in the future. You get to choose whether you allow Him to.

I understand how hard it can be to get past the person you no longer want to be. And when you feel as if you've failed God, seeing past that failure can seem almost impossible. I really believe the first step to enjoying your life is to approach God with what you feel is too painful to even talk about. Perhaps you're ashamed, and you don't want to bring it up. Just the thought of admitting it to God causes a knot to form in your stomach.

I hate to burst your bubble, but…He already knows. He is asking you to say it out loud. And I honestly believe when you hear yourself say it, you are more likely to make a correction.

Talking to God about the limits you have put around your life is also the best way to learn to lean on Him. If you don't believe you need someone like God to lean on, you will live a tired life. Plus, if you can forgive yourself, the people around you will notice, and they will forgive you as well. I can tell you firsthand what it is like when you turn everything over to God: It's like a huge burden gets lifted off your shoulders, and now you're ready to stop existing and start living.

Now to him who is able to do immeasurably more than all we ask or imagine, according to his power that is at work within us...
EPHESIANS 3:20

ANCHOR POINTS

- In a healthy family, everyone feels heard, supported, and cared for, even when there is a disagreement.
- Life doesn't care what your deer scores.
- God wants you to depend on, recognize, worship, and love Him.
- Life isn't about sulking over what you don't have, but enjoying what you do have while waiting for what you want.
- It's impossible to enjoy where you are if you feel that you owe God a debt you can't repay.

CONFESSION FIRE

As Karin suggested, make a list of things you value most in life. Once you've compiled a list of five or six items that are important to you, ask yourself, Which of these are getting the most attention, and which are getting none? What will you do to fix this?

KARIN'S GAME PLAN

WILD TURKEY GARLIC MEATBALLS WITH ZUCCHINI NOODLES

INGREDIENTS

8 oz. raw ground turkey
¼ cup reduced-fat mozzarella cheese
½ tsp. garlic powder
¼ tsp. dried basil
¼ tsp. dried oregano
1 cube bouillon
½ cup cilantro (chopped)
¼ tsp. salt
¼ tsp. black pepper
1 T. butter
1 T. lemon juice
1 T. Frank's Hot Sauce
2½ cups zucchini noodles

DIRECTIONS

1. In a large bowl, combine the ground turkey, cheese, half of the garlic powder, basil, oregano, bouillon cube, chopped cilantro, salt, and black pepper. Mix well with your hands or a fork and form into medium balls. Arrange on a plate and set aside.

2. Spray a large skillet with Pam and place over medium-low heat. Cook the meatballs for 8 to 10 minutes on all sides, until browned and cooked through. While cooking, baste the meatballs with the juices. Remove to a clean plate and set aside.

3. In the same skillet, melt the butter. Add lemon juice, hot sauce, and the rest of the garlic powder. Add the zucchini noodles and cook for 3 or 4 minutes, stirring regularly until zucchini is done but still crisp and the juices have reduced a bit.

4. Push zucchini to the side of the skillet and add the meatballs back to the pan. Reheat. Serve immediately. Enjoy!

NUTRITION

Serving size—2 meatballs
Calories—78
Fat—2.6 grams
Carbohydrates—4.2 grams
Protein—9.7 grams

12

POP

A Tribute to David's Dad

DAVID | My first deer hunt was with my dad. Every boy should be so lucky. As I've already said, Dad wasn't much for deer hunting, preferring to stay back at camp and cook for the rest of us. However, when I was ten years old, he wasn't about to let me hunt by myself or even go with one of my uncles. He would be the one to introduce me to the deer and the woods. In my family, deer hunting was all about the men getting away and camping for a few days. Back then, tents were horrible, so we usually rented pop-up campers. At that time in Virginia, deer season lasted for two weeks, and the last day was doe day.

On opening morning, Dad and I got up early to go on our first hunt. I wanted to go as far back into the woods as possible because I believed all the big deer lived there. Dad, on the other hand, wasn't comfortable hiking through unfamiliar territory. Against his better judgment, we walked a good way back into the timber to a spot where the ridge we were on overlooked a valley. I spotted a spike walking parallel to us on the next ridge, about 100 yards away. It took some doing, but I was finally able to point it out to my dad.

Once he saw it, he had me sit down, brace up, and take a shot with my 410. To this day, I can still remember the leaves flying up about four feet below the deer. I had shot well underneath the buck. Dad took the next shot with his 12-gauge, and the deer immediately hit the ground, staggered back up, and ran away. We weren't sure what had happened, as neither of us were experienced deer hunters.

After looking around, but finding no trace of the deer, Dad was convinced it had just slipped and fallen. As I look back, I'm not sure that was the case. I'm not even sure we reached the spot where the deer fell because we never found signs of a hit or the deer itself. This proves how out of his element my dad really was that day. The only reason he was in those woods was that he had a ten-year-old son who loved hunting.

It was time to go back to camp, but my dad was looking a little turned around. Finally, he glanced over his shoulder and asked me, "What ridge did we walk in on?" I didn't know either. Dad was getting nervous. He asked me to climb a tree to see if I could get a better vantage point of where we were. In Dad's mind, we were lost. As I climbed, I looked up the hill and saw a truck drive by. We were less than 100 yards from the main road.

I look back now and realize how horrible my dad must have felt. He was trying to be a good dad by taking his son hunting, and he ended up getting lost. To this day, I feel bad for my dad because he was only trying to do something he wasn't good at, for the sake of his son.

I also now realize how great that day really was. My dad was doing something for me that he had absolutely no desire to do. He couldn't care less if he hunted or not, but he did care that I liked to hunt. He was willing to get way out of his comfort zone for my sake. I've tried to be that kind of dad to Warren and Easton. I hope the mark I leave on them will be as deep as the mark my dad left on me.

ON THE HUNT

For this particular hunt, we had traveled with the boys to Arkansas to go duck hunting. And as I stared at the 12-gauge leaning against the duck blind, I couldn't help but think about my own dad and the story this gun might tell others about his life. If that 12-gauge could speak, its story might go something like this:

> In 1963 I was issued to a police officer. He was taught how to respect me. In 30 years of service, that officer carried me on hundreds of calls, yet we never fired at anyone. Years later that same officer taught his son, David, how to properly use me. David carried me on more hunting trips than I can possibly remember, and just like his father, he taught his sons how to handle me. Those boys, Warren and Easton, have been carrying me on hunting trips ever since.

Earlier that morning, my boys had been standing on the shoreline of an Arkansas swamp, about to share a moment hunting ducks with their parents. Yet it felt insignificant. None of it seemed like a big deal. And it wasn't…until you realize what had brought them to that moment. It started with their parents sharing their adventures with them, but when you add two dogs, two boats, and too much gear, what you get are two trips to the duck blind. None of us were complaining

Three generations of hunting Holders. Pictured (from left) are Warren, Easton, Pop, and David.

though. How could we on such a beautiful morning? We were all there for the same reason—to witness the raw beauty of a cold winter sun rising over a flooded marsh. But we had not just come to see this beauty. We were there to touch, taste, hear, and smell it. More than that, we had come to be a part of it. Our boat ride took us to a duck blind where two things led our family to realize that there can never be too many ways to leave your mark.

On this hunt, so much would be the same, and yet so much would be different. We were in the same place as last year, with the same friends, and even in the same duck blind. For me, the reason it felt different this time was that my dad couldn't come with us. At 81, he simply wasn't healthy enough.

As Karin, Warren, Easton, and I were watching for ducks, my mind drifted back to my dad's shotgun, the one leaning against the blind. It had been in our family for more than 50 years. Every scratch stood for something, just like the deep mark Pop had left on Easton's gun the year before. You see, Pop shot a duck in this very same spot on our last trip. Right after that, he dropped the gun, leaving a thick mark in the wood. I had no idea at the time how much that mark would come to mean to all of us. Every time I look at it, I'm reminded of my dad and the last hunting trip he would ever take with our family. And the only one where all three generations would be present.

On this day, however, the duck hunting was slow, but it never really mattered. This duck blind was equipped with a full kitchen, so the smell of bacon, along with the company of good friends, made the hunt special before any of us ever fired a shot. When the ducks came in, Karin killed her first bird, and the best part was that she had killed it with Dad's gun. If a good duck hunt is measured by how many shells you shoot, we were having a blast. Or perhaps killing only one duck for every ten that came in was just our way of leaving our own mark and making our own memories. Later, with Easton sleeping, Warren texting, me out of shells, and the sun about to set, it was time to go home.

Another year and another duck hunt had come and gone. As much as I try to hold on, the hunts keep coming and going. They seem to get faster every year. I'm left trying to understand and to teach my boys that no matter how simple or small something seems, we won't know how important it was until after it has happened. That moment on the shoreline is etched into my brain more than my boys will ever understand. Seeing them there without Pop was a harsh reminder that life continues with or without us.

The moments that mean the most are usually the ones we've been taking for granted. Once, Pop was here, making memories with us on this same duck hunt. Today, my dad is in heaven. Though he's no longer with us, we're still here to make sure that

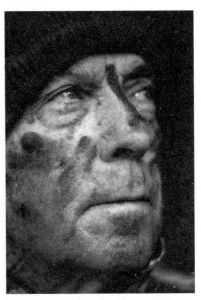

Pop Holder, a 38-year veteran of the police force, made many sacrifices for his family.

marks like his are never forgotten. This trip wasn't about my dad getting sick, the time he won't be spending here on earth with his two favorite grandsons, or how much we will miss him on all our hunting adventures. It wasn't even about his gun or the mark he left on Easton's. It was about him leaving his mark on all of us.

Some moments in your life stand out above others. These are the moments you'll do just about anything to preserve. To me, it seems the longer you try to hang on to them, the more they seem to get lost in the day-to-day shuffle. Still, you hang on. I think the bigger question is, Why? Why do you hang on—and why do some moments in life mean more than others? For me, it's about who was present with me in the moment. That last duck hunt with my dad will always be preserved in my heart and mind. I've been lucky enough to share many similar moments with Karin, Warren, and Easton. Life isn't about where you go or what you do. It's about who goes with you and the memories you make with those you love. We love you, Pop. Thank you for the memories and the marks you left on all of us.

BEYOND THE HUNT

I think my relationship with my dad was typical. When I was a kid, he worked a lot, serving on the police force for 38 years. At the time, we lived just outside of Washington, DC, in northern Virginia. Police officers don't make a lot of money, so for my mom to stay home with me, Dad had to work two or three jobs. With him always working, Mom was the one taking me to practices and sporting events.

Dad sacrificed a lot for our family. As a result, I didn't get to do much with him when I was growing up. However, when I did get to spend time with him on a family fishing or hunting trip, he was the life of the party. Dad was a lot of fun and loved telling stories. By the time I became a teenager, though, his absence began to show up in my behavior. I ran around with my friends, getting into all kinds of mischief. Without him there to correct me, I only got worse.

Like most dads, my dad was doing what he thought was best for me by working to provide for our family, so I never held that against him. But I was determined not to be absent from Warren's and Easton's lives, no matter what. That determination was one very good reason to pursue a career I could share with my family rather than one that would take me away from them.

Even though Dad wasn't a big hunter, he supported my passion for hunting. When I got my first compound bow, he asked me all kinds of questions about how to hunt with it. Back in the 1980s, there weren't many bowhunters, so there wasn't a lot of information out there about the sport. Dad and I may not have been extremely close as I was growing into a man, but I could always count on him. If I needed something, he was willing to drop whatever he was doing to help.

Not long after I moved out of my parents' house, my older brother committed suicide. It tore my dad apart. Karin and I were engaged at the time, but with everything going on, we called off the wedding and even stopped dating. Shortly after that, I decided I had to move, so I went to Karin and told her I was going to Arkansas. She went with me, and we got married. The job waiting for me in Arkansas fell through, so I applied at the fire department and was hired.

That job brought my dad and me back together. He was so proud to have a son working as a firefighter, and it didn't hurt that I quickly made lieutenant. Once we moved to Montana and I was made captain, he and Mom flew out for the ceremony. He was as excited for me as when I started working for Primos Hunting. Eventually, Mom and Dad moved to Montana, where Karin and I were living. (I think the fact that we had their only grandkids might have played a role in that.) Dad began traveling with me around the country as I presented seminars on elk hunting. He was proud to be a part of those, and prouder of the fact that I was his son.

Dad passed away in 2018 from Alzheimer's. I really miss him. He was a big part of our lives the last few years. I was there when he took his last breath, and I knew it would be his last. As Mom and I sat by his bedside at the VA hospital, a flood of memories went through my mind. At that moment, all the things that went right and all the things that went wrong in our relationship no longer mattered. He wasn't perfect, but he instilled in me a set of values that have guided me my entire life.

If he were still here, he would tell you the biggest achievement in his life wasn't something that happened on the police force, but the day he became a grandpa. He loved my two boys more than anyone could imagine. He was around for them as they were growing up more than he was able to be when I was. I'm okay with that. Warren and Easton got to enjoy Pop, and any time he missed spending with me he more than made up for with them. To me, that means everything.

That's the mark I'm referring to. The mark you leave on someone's soul. When the memory of another person has been etched into your heart, you're never really without them. Pop taught us all more than we knew when he was with us, and he is still teaching. He taught me that when you walk into a room, the people in that room should be happy to have met you, and that when you leave a room, it should be better than when you found it. It doesn't matter if it's a 12-by-12 office or God's big room we call the outdoors. I learned that from Ted Holder, and my boys…well, they learned it from Pop.

KARIN | I think the thing I loved most about Pop was his joyfulness and sense of kindness. He was the sort of man who did not like conflict and who would use humor to avoid confrontation. He often poked fun instead of getting angry. I've always found that interesting because he was in law enforcement. His career took up most of his time when David was a boy, so later in life he dedicated himself to our boys. He took them on daily Walmart runs and made sure they had turkey-bacon sandwiches after school. Pop was there for all their sporting events and school activities and even some hunting, though hunting wasn't really his thing. If it meant getting to spend time with David and the boys, Pop was in. He didn't really care what they were doing if they were together. Just as he had scratched the stock of Easton's brand-new shotgun in the duck blind, he left a mark on everyone's heart, a mark that will never be forgotten.

Not every person you meet is going to leave a mark like Pop. However, there are special connections and relationships you develop over the years that will imprint themselves on you forever. You'll know when you have a relationship like that with someone in your life because he or she will help make you complete; will make you the best version of yourself. The right people will pray for you and have your back—and you will do the same for them. These people, like Pop, will understand you and accept you for who you are. They are with you even if you haven't seen them in years. People like that are special in life and should never be taken for granted.

As for Pop, we will miss him terribly. However, we are comforted, knowing he is with our Lord and Savior. Pop has made it to his new home and is at peace. David, his mom, and I will press on, as will Warren and Easton. The mark he left on all of us would be wasted if we didn't pass on the lessons he taught us.

Honor your father and your mother, so that you may live long in the land the LORD your God is giving you.
EXODUS 20:12

ANCHOR POINTS

- Life on earth is temporary, so leave a deep mark.
- The moments and the marks that mean the most are usually the ones we've taken for granted.
- When the memory of another person has been etched onto your heart, you're never really without them.
- Time spent together as a family is never wasted.

CONFESSION FIRE

Just as Pop left his mark on us, you will leave your mark on those closest to you. Consider the things about yourself that you hope to pass on. How could you do an even better job leaving your mark?

KARIN'S GAME PLAN

GARLIC BASIL ROASTED PHEASANT

INGREDIENTS

1 pheasant
1 T. crushed garlic
black pepper to taste
¼ cup basil olive oil

DIRECTIONS

1. Preheat oven to 350 degrees.

2. Position full pheasant in a roasting dish, breast-side up.

3. Mix the seasonings in a bowl and brush the mixture over the top of the bird.

4. Cover with aluminum foil.

5. Bake 20 minutes, rotate, and bake for another 20 minutes.

6. Remove the foil and put back in the oven for another 10 minutes or until golden brown.

NUTRITION

Serving size—1 pheasant breast (4 oz.)
Calories—154
Fat—4 grams
Carbohydrates—0 grams
Protein—28 grams

CONCLUSION

DAVID | It's hard to believe I'm already writing the conclusion when I feel as if I just started. But then again, that's life. When you're young, you can't wait until you're older, and once you're older, you can't figure out how to stop life from moving so fast. It's like you're holding on to a rope that's dragging you down a hill. You're trying to let go but can't, so it just keeps pulling you.

I'm honored you picked up this book and took this journey with us. I hope we've helped you in some way, big or small. What you might not be aware of, though, is that you've helped me too. Just sharing the *Raised Hunting* story with you has reminded me that we don't have all the answers—and that we don't *need* all the answers. All you and I really need is someone bigger than us to believe in and lean on. As I've looked back and considered how blessed my family has been, my relationship with God has gotten stronger. I hope you realize that just as God has been there for my family, He is equally there for you and yours. Even when I didn't recognize what was happening, God was turning my life into something incredible. I've learned that you don't have to question God; you just need to trust Him.

Before writing this book, I wasn't sure I had much of a message to share—at least not one I thought others would be interested in. I believed I was just living life. Now I understand that everything our family has experienced, from our hunting show to our hunting camps, has God's fingerprints all over it. This is not a fictional place or fantasy land that I've been sharing with you; there really is a life at full draw, even if that life looks different for each of us.

I don't want you to close this book and think that I have all the answers. I don't. Nor have I dealt with all the issues that are currently still on the table. I'm a regular guy with a big God leading the way. Finding God's plan for your life isn't always simple, and that's why few seem to find it. I hope that by reading our story, you will begin to look for your life at full draw.

We get one chance to live on this earth, and I'm unwilling to waste it. I can't begin to explain to you how much I love the outdoors. Hunting is something I don't think everyone understands. It's about more than just killing animals, putting meat in your freezer, hanging a trophy on the wall, or gaining bragging rights. It's an opportunity to learn ethics, values, responsibility, and determination.

Just like in life, when you walk out into a hunt, you don't know what's coming. You only know that whatever happens, you have a responsibility to the animal and yourself to handle every situation

David and Karin Holder (and Old Dan) pose with the elusive deer known as the Big Eight.

correctly. That's a life at full draw. A life that says, "I'm going to do the right thing even when no one else is looking."

I love helping people. So if I can help you into the woods or into God's kingdom, that's all any man like me can ask. I'm 50 years old, but I'm nowhere close to done! I still have a lot of life left to live. So do you. I'm glad God included you on this journey, and I look forward to our future adventures together. We're changing lives one arrow at a time.

KARIN | From the depths of my soul, I cannot thank you enough for taking the time to read this book. If I can help you avoid some of the heartbreaking mistakes I've made over time, whether in life or in the woods, I'm happy to do that. I'm willing to share my mistakes and some of my worst moments with you only because, like you, I'm human. I'm also happy to have shared some of our best experiences, and 99 percent of the time in the Holder family, those moments happen on our outdoor adventures. Whether we are in a deer stand or hiking through the mountains, outside is where my family connects and recharges our relationships. It's also the place where I spend time in prayer, connecting with our heavenly Father.

Most of all, I hope some of the takeaways you have received from these stories are to never give up, to define your purpose, and to believe God has specifically designed a life at full draw for you.

With God at your side, anything is possible. You can face the ups and downs of both the hunt and life with an attitude of gratefulness, realizing it's okay to let go of some of the things that are dragging you down and away from God's purpose. For me, my faith has been the foundation of everything I do in life. Faith has always been my answer. I'm still learning and growing in my walk with God, but I do know that without His help, I wouldn't be where I am today.

If you are not an outdoors person, I hope this book has shown you how the outdoors and the culture of hunting are good things. Hunting is necessary for the balance of God's creation. Perhaps the Holder family has shown you a different side of hunting, one that the media does not like to share. For David, Warren, Easton, and me, hunting is our connection to each other and the world around us. And we hope we've connected with you as well. My prayer for you is that our stories, the journey we've taken, and the recipes I have shared will nourish your family, feed your soul, and encourage you to plan your next hunting adventure.

I wish you well in life and on the hunt. May you find yourself at full draw in both!

We know that in all things God works for the good of those who love him, who have been called according to his purpose.

ROMANS 8:28

To learn more about Harvest House books and
to read sample chapters, visit our website:

www.harvesthousepublishers.com

HARVEST HOUSE PUBLISHERS
EUGENE, OREGON